UNSEEN EARNHARDT

THE MAN BEHIND THE MASK

3

EDITED BY LEE KLANCHER

MBI Publishing Company

First published in 2002 by MBI Publishing Company,
Galtier Plaza, Suite 200, 380 Jackson Street,
St. Paul, MN 55101-3885 USA

MBI Publishing Company books are also available at discounts in bulk quantity for industrial or sales-promotional use. For details write to Special Sales Manager at Motorbooks International Wholesalers & Distributors, Galtier Plaza, Suite 200, 380 Jackson Street, St. Paul, MN 55101-3885 USA.

Library of Congress Cataloging-in-Publication Data Available

ISBN 0-7603-1391-1

On the front cover: By the end of 2000, Earnhardt was showing evidence of 25 years in the toughest business on earth, but to the very end he never showed an ounce of give. Framed here at Rockingham that October, his eyes reveal that experience as he prepares for another sundown battle with points leader Bobby Labonte. Labonte finished 20th, but Earnhardt did not gain much ground in the title chase, finishing 17th. *Nigel Kinrade*

On the frontispiece: A lighter side shows through before the start of the 1999 Las Vegas 400. In typical late-career fashion, Earnhardt charged from the 38th starting position to finish seventh in the race. *Nigel Kinrade*

On the title page: Earnhardt charges off the track and into the garage during practice at Rockingham in February, the week after the Daytona 500. Wrecked out of a chance at victory at Daytona, Earnhardt's yearlong losing streak had reached 28. Things got no better at The Rock, with Earnhardt finishing 11th. *Nigel Kinrade*

On the back cover: Earnhardt acknowledges the crowd during driver introductions prior to the start of the 2001 Daytona 500. *Nigel Kinrade*

Edited by Lee Klancher
Designed by Tom Heffron

Printed in China

CONTENTS

INTRODUCTION

By Lee Klancher

One of the great racing stories of our time is that of Dale Earnhardt, a man driven to be the best at what he did. For 23 years, Dale's determination and audacity made him the most polarizing driver on the NASCAR circuit. When Dale died, the entire country mourned his passing, and his story transcended racing to become a part of the American lexicon.

In the air-conditioned McTownhouse that comprises today's typical American life, Dale Earnhardt was a breath of fresh country air. He spoke his mind, wasn't afraid to swagger, and raced fast cars hard. He also had a lot of money and grabbed our time's cultural brass ring: fame. During a time when the vast majority of Americans were afraid to speak up about an overcooked steak, Dale's primal life appealed to everyone from the good ol' girls and boys to neck-tied cubicle dwellers.

In *Unseen Earnhardt*, some of the great stories about Dale are brought to life. Rather than exhaustively covering the man's career, the book offers glimpses into aspects of Earnhardt that haven't been seen and aren't well-known.

The Dale Earnhardt story is made more interesting by the fact that he personified his sport during an era of tremendous change in NASCAR. He burst upon the scene in 1979, a time that writer Al Pearce credits as the birthdate of big-time NASCAR racing. That year's Daytona 500 was a drama-filled event that captured the hearts and minds of the American television audience. Dale wasn't a factor in that race, but it was the year that he quickly emerged as the hot new star in this growing sport.

In these pages, you can see just how the sport's evolution changed the men and situations of NASCAR. Just one look at Dale and Teresa relaxing on lawn chairs in the back of a box van in the late 1980s is enough to make it clear to even the most peripheral fan how far Winston Cup racing has come. A walk through any pit lane on the circuit today—with drivers sequestered in mammoth motorhomes or surrounded by crowds of lackeys and fans—makes it hard to believe that kind of grassroots environment existed only 15 or 20 years ago.

The book is organized by periods of Dale's racing career, starting with his pre-Winston Cup career. From there, it is organized by owners, with the long stretch of years he drove for Richard Childress divided up by his crew chiefs.

Photography takes center stage in this book, and the bulk of the book is pulled from three amazing collections.

Bryant McMurray's four-decade career in motorsports has taken him from regional tracks—like Metrolina Speedway near Charlotte—to F1 races in Europe. He's also worked for STP and as the director of operations for the first-ever NASCAR race outside of the U.S., a 1989 event in Melbourne, Australia.

Dick Conway began his motorsports career in photography and currently has an extensive archive chronicling the mid 1970s through the early 1990s. He has supplied photographs to *The Richmond News Leader* and *Autoweek*.

From about 1992 forward, most of the photographs bear the credit of **Nigel Kinrade**, a regular in *Racer* magazine and other publications, and one of today's most talented race phototographers.

While this is a photo-oriented book, the text is far from incidental. Three racing journalists uncovered new and interesting takes on each period of Dale's career, and what they found adds some great reading to this photo history.

Racing journalist **Jonathan Ingram** found the debt Dale owed to Petty Engineering for helping him get started in his Winston Cup career, the real story of the now infamous Pink Car, and much more. As a side note, you'll notice that the opening chapter has two stories. That is due to things we won't mention in print—let's just say that I, as the editor, now owe Jonathan a beer or two.

Writer **Al Pearce** told the story of what he considered one of the most significant points of Dale's career, his win at Bristol in his rookie season. Always the master of his trade, Al also was able to find a fresh angle on Dale's historic win at the Daytona 500.

Few people were closer to Bud Moore than writer **David Green**, who chronicled a race in which Dale's car was less than he hoped, and how he nursed a fragile powertrain through a tough race at Darlington.

Racer magazine correspondent **Ben Blake** penned captions and organized photographs for the project, and brought his take to the story of Dale Earnhardt.

Working with this group of talented journalists has been a privilege and a joy. The photos that turned up have been fascinating to see. The visual record alone is enough to show how Dale progressed from a brash and intense young racer to the accomplished professional of his later days. And the stories were a pleasure to read and edit.

I hope you enjoy this book and find the discoveries contained inside as enjoyable to nd view as they were for me to hunt down.

read a

THE PINK CAR

By Jonathan Ingram

The man who would one day become known as "The Intimidator" driving black cars in the Winston Cup began his career in a most unlikely machine. At the Concord Motor Speedway, just down the road from his home in Kannapolis, North Carolina, Dale Earnhardt drove his first race aboard a 1955 Ford with a pink body and a top painted an equally bizarre color—apricot metal flake.

Earnhardt's inaugural ride in 1971 at the age of 20 didn't fit the family's racing reputation, which had been established by his father Ralph, much less Dale's own future image as a driver unwilling to give any quarter. This borrowed jalopy with a V-6 engine symbolized the determination for which its driver would become well known. Earnhardt wasn't going to let a car's oddball status at the local dirt track stand in the way of getting his first ride.

THE EARLY DAYS

His blowtorch intense desire to become a race car driver—and the fact he had no money—easily overcame any reservation Earnhardt had about driving the pink car loaned to him by friend and brother-in-law David Oliver. A high school dropout who had been through one divorce and was already remarried, Earnhardt had precious few means to display his ambitions, much less find out about his ability. His father Ralph, the NASCAR Late Model Champion in 1956 and a well-known short-track ace, wasn't about to help him get started. He believed his son should make his own way.

Ralph Earnhardt raced immaculately prepared white cars, numbered 8, that were driven with the same precision the owner put into building them. Willing to run close and hard, the older Earnhardt terrorized drivers and frustrated Carolina promoters with his consistency. Occasionally, the people running the show had to put a bounty on Earnhardt's head to attract drivers who could beat him and thereby stir up ticket buyers' interest.

"Ralph was probably the best I've ever seen," said Oliver, a neighbor of the Earnhardts who would go on to become a shop foreman for Roush Racing's Winston Cup cars. "Ralph would build his own car from the ground up, build his own motors. Then he'd get in it and outrun you. There were not many at that time who could do that—and nobody can do it any more."

A good family man with two daughters who were followed by three sons, Ralph Earnhardt had plenty of friends and admirers in the pits but when it came to racing, he was a lone wolf, intent on winning enough short-track races to feed his family and sustain himself as a full-time racer.

Quiet and focused, Ralph Earnhardt stuck to his own methods. He would sometimes wake up in the middle of the night, go out to his garage behind the house on the corner

Earnhardt made his first Winston Cup start in Charlotte's World 600 on May 25, 1975, in the No. 8 Dodge owned by Ed Negre. There was still plenty of room for young hopefuls in the 1970s. Here, Earnhardt, who started 33rd and finished 22nd, leads the No. 05 car of David Sisco.
Bryant McMurray

Page 9: Earnhardt zips by the flagstand as caution flies during a 1974 Sportsman race at Metrolina. The No. 8 was the same as that driven by Dale's father, Ralph Earnhardt, national Sportsman champ in 1956. Ralph Earnhardt died suddenly in 1973.
Bryant McMurray

of Coach and Sedan at the edge of the mill town of Kannapolis, and work on the car, pursuing an idea while it was still fresh. His intensity sometimes made him seem cold and aloof.

"You'd walk into his garage and he'd be working on a motor and wouldn't even acknowledge you," said Oliver. "I remember I went by there one time and sat around for about ten minutes and then got up to leave. Ralph said, 'Where you going?' I told him if he wasn't going to say anything I might as well leave. He said, 'David, if I talked to everybody who came in this garage, I'd never get any work done.'"

The work of maintaining and then racing cars several times a week during the season stretched from early spring until late fall for the senior Earnhardt. During the winters, in the time-honored method of the Carolinas, Earnhardt mapped out the frames for his cars in the hard clay floor of his garage, then built them literally from the ground up with a welding torch. Likewise, he put his engines together from scratch. He sometimes

Earnhardt also tried out the big track at Charlotte in the more-familiar Sportsman cars. In the fall 1976 race, Earnhardt pushes the family No. 8 through the first and second turns in the late laps. *Bryant McMurray*

repaired cars during the winter to make ends meet. This brutal workload led to his fatal heart attack at the age of 45.

The oldest of three sons, Dale was a vital part of his father's racing while growing up. Ralph sometimes carried his oldest and most eager boy, plus neighbor Oliver, to the track. Once there, Dale pestered some of the veteran racers in the pits to buy him hot dogs before hopping on the back of his father's truck to watch the main feature.

THE EARLY DAYS

As he grew older, Dale became a regular in his father's garage in the evenings—at the expense of his schoolwork. Even while in classes, Earnhardt spent more time thinking about getting home to count the dents in his father's car after a weeknight short-track race than thinking about his schoolwork. For a teenage boy who never felt comfortable in school, it was a way of compensating, according to classmate Richard Sowers, who would later revive his friendship with Earnhardt while working as a public relations representative in the Winston Cup.

"When things don't come easily to you, which I don't think they did for Dale at that age," said Sowers, "then it's easier to say forget the academics or baseball practice or play practice. By the age of 14 or 15, he was spending four or five hours a night helping his father in the shop."

"I tried every way I could to get Dale to stay in school," said Oliver, a three-letter man in football, wrestling, and baseball. "I'd take him with me to wrestling matches to try to get him interested in something that would help him stay in school. But his heart was already set on being a race car driver."

With his mind made up about his racing ambitions, Dale quit school at age 16 despite the fact his father was dead-set against it. The decision began a rift with Ralph

The driver introductions at the fall 1977 Charlotte race, then called the National 500, were elaborate. Earnhardt, preparing to make his first Cup start of the year, runs the red carpet. The race was forgettable, with Dale falling out on the 25th lap due to mechanical trouble with Henley Gray's back-mark car. *Bryant McMurray*

that lasted until Dale was able to find his own way into the racing business. "Dale knew that Ralph was not pleased with him for quitting school," said Oliver. "Ralph didn't try to hide his feelings. He voiced his displeasure and then went on. He wanted his son to have an education."

When Dale married at age 18—against his father's wishes once again—the rift deepened. Dale moved away from home, had his first son, Kerry, and spent less time at the shop. The marriage failed in part because Earnhardt's wife didn't understand his obsession with

THE EARLY DAYS

trying to go racing and holding down a job as a welder. The day he received his divorce papers, Earnhardt married again, but this time he married into racing. He wed Brenda Gee, the daughter of Robert Gee, a dirt-track car owner. Even with a new wife, one aspect of his life remained constant: the only thing dimmer than his prospects for income were his prospects for making a living as a race car driver.

Dale was hardly following the example of his father, whose values were as clear as frame rails mapped out in the hard clay. Ralph made a stable family life a priority. He raced successfully enough to feed a family of five children and forsook a Winston Cup career due to the financial risk of racing the superspeedways.

Not surprisingly, when a still-destitute Dale and his friend David went to Ralph and asked permission for the 20-year-old to drive the pink machine at the Concord track, the senior Earnhardt remained unconvinced. He reminded Oliver that he would not agree to fix the car if his son wrecked it.

Earnhardt had attracted enough attention by 1978 to run some of the bigger races of the summer, beginning with the World 600 in Will Cronkite's No. 96. Here, he steers the blue-and-white Ford in the outside lane, just behind the No. 3 car of another independent: a fellow named Richard Childress. *Bryant McMurray*

"Ralph was not a real compassionate man," said Oliver. "He made Dale work for his own cars and reach his goals on his own."

Oliver was the original pilot of the pink car, which drew a few wisecracks at the track. The pink paint was mixed by a local speed shop owner and sponsor, who concocted it in an effort to come up with something that complemented the apricot metal-flake roof, which had been chosen with the hope it would show up well underneath the Concord track's lights. When Oliver got an offer to drive elsewhere, the machine, which

A RACER'S EGO

By Jonathan Ingram

Tex Powell had the unique experience of working with a shy 22-year-old Dale Earnhardt who took part in an impromptu factory test day and later when he was an accomplished Winston Cup champion. "Every time Dale would win a championship with Childress, he would have commemorative pocketknives made," said Powell, whose company built the transmissions for Richard Childress Racing. "The next season, he wouldn't say much, just walk by and jam one in your pocket."

Still more of a man of action than words, it was all too obvious that Earnhardt overcame his shyness after he became established in the Winston Cup. "He reminded me a lot of working with A. J. Foyt. They both had similar racers' egos," said Powell. "I mean, you have to have a big ego to be successful as a race car driver. If I wanted to get something on the car for A. J. or Dale, I had to approach it as if it was their idea. I'd say, 'You remember when you said you thought this would be a good idea?' They'd say, 'Oh yeah, let's go ahead and do that.'"

Powell recalled a day at the Sears Point Raceway road course when Earnhardt complained that the transmission wasn't going into second gear. "I leaned in the passenger-side window and I noticed that a flange had been added to the seat to protect his right leg in case of an accident. I said, 'Dale, I think the problem is the seat. You're moving your leg in the corners while you're shifting and it's preventin' you from getting the car in second gear.'"

Earnhardt shot back his reply. "I ain't moving my leg in the corners! I keep it straight." He then left the pits. When he returned, through the driver's side window, Earnhardt shouted to his pit crew. "You guys need to get in here and fix this seat. It won't let me get into second gear."

After completing 382 tough laps and finishing 17th at the World 600 in 1978, Earnhardt showed disappointment and fatigue. Next time out, however, he notched a career-best seventh place in the Firecracker at Daytona, and others began to take notice. *Bryant McMurray*

was numbered K-2 (at the time, so many cars showed up for dirt-track races that numbers were joined with the first letter of the driver's hometown), became available.

Oliver's father Ray actually owned the car and gave the young Earnhardt the same advice he'd given his own son when David had started to race. "You need to just fall in and follow," said Ray. "That way you can learn how to race. If you don't do that, then you can learn how to build cars. Because when you wreck the cars, you have to fix them."

Earnhardt initially agreed to this strategy, but just as he had already proven he was stubborn and hard-headed about doing things his own way in dealing with his father, he eventually had ideas different from those of Ray Oliver. Once he got behind the wheel of the pink car and was prepared to race, Earnhardt leaned his head out the window and said to one of the volunteer crewmen, "Could you ask Ray if it would be okay to pass a couple of cars?"

The results may not have been earthshaking, but Earnhardt never wrecked the pink car. And it wasn't just the paint job that drew attention to him. The quiet young man of few words had a locally famous name. "Everybody around Kannapolis and Concord knew Ralph Earnhardt was an outstanding race car driver," said Sowers. It was only natural that fans and other team owners paid attention to his son, who quickly showed signs of success. After several months of running in the weekly semi-modified class races aboard K-2, Earnhardt started getting offers from other local car owners, first James Miller, and then Tommy Russell.

Dale's stubborn stick-to-it-iveness and inaugural success impressed another car owner—Ralph Earnhardt. Once it became clear that his prodigal son was determined to race and find his own way, the senior Earnhardt began to give Dale the sort of priceless advice born out of his own experience. Just as he had shown Dale the finer points of how to weld cars, hang bodies, and build engines while they worked together in his garage, Ralph began teaching him how to get around the track faster, time his overtaking maneuvers, and how to protect himself from a driver bent on trying to spin him out.

"Sometimes Ralph would sit us down in the garage and take a welding rod, draw a track in the dirt, and then show us where we needed to be," said Oliver. "Then you'd get on the track and do things like he told you and what he said would happen is what happened."

Dale himself never tired of telling the story of the time his father pushed him to victory in one of his early races at Concord, where sometimes the semi-modified V-6 entries ran with the Late Model V-8s to fill out the field on the half-mile oval. "I was running second in the cars with V-6 engines and Daddy was leading in the Late Models. He come up behind me and started pushing me down the straightaways," Dale would recall. "That helped me catch the guy who was leading and win."

The second-generation driver would tell the story regularly over the years with the same happy recollection. That race, more than anything else, confirmed his baptism as a racer. It acknowledged that his father, heroic to him in so many ways, had accepted Dale's decision to follow his own difficult road as a race car driver. In the tumultuous years after Ralph's death in 1973, the younger Earnhardt banked on the knowledge that he had his father's blessing, as well as his talent.

It all began in that pink Ford with an apricot metal-flake top and "K-2" on the door. "Even then you could see it in him," said Oliver. "Dale was going to be something special. He would take a tenth-place car and finish fifth. It wasn't long before he could take a fifth-place car and finish first."

Thus continued a family tradition in a car the same color as a newborn baby.

First Factory Ride

By Jonathan Ingram

When Dale Earnhardt stood at the podium in the main ballroom of the jam-packed Waldorf Astoria to accept his seventh Winston Cup championship in 1994, he mentioned a lot of people who had helped him achieve his goal of matching the same number of titles as "The King," Richard Petty. Earnhardt thanked Petty, in fact, and several others for giving him his "first factory ride" 20 years earlier.

A lot of other names were mentioned, but it seemed strange that Earnhardt would talk about a factory ride from the mid-1970s, when Petty Engineering was in its prime and The King won four Winston Cups in five seasons with Chrysler products. Nobody could remember Dale Earnhardt—or even Ralph Earnhardt, a legend on Carolina short tracks—aboard a Chrysler, Dodge, or Plymouth. But Earnhardt also thanked Larry Rathgeb, the engineer for Chrysler and its Mopar products during the roaring 1960s, and Pete Hamilton, famed for driving a Petty-blue Plymouth Superbird into victory lane at the Daytona 500 in 1970. He also thanked Tex Powell, whose career as a drivetrain guru started at Petty Enterprises.

Earnhardt first met all three of these men early in 1974 on a still day at an otherwise vacant Concord Speedway. Rathgeb had with him a brand-new Chrysler dubbed the "Kit Car." This was the first of the cars destined for short tracks all over the U.S. under various sanctions had black primer for paint and an inauspicious "0" on the door. Otherwise, it might as well have been a grocery getter.

This was an important project for Rathgeb, an expert chassis engineer charged with getting the Chrysler name established on short tracks and keeping the Mopar aftermarket business up to speed in light of the withdrawal of direct factory involvement in the Winston Cup. "We didn't have a whole lot of dollars and we needed to get some drivers winning races with a program that at least paid for itself," he said.

The Chrysler Kit Car would eventually prove successful because a driver could build the car himself from a kit, add a Mopar V-8, and win races. Prior to that day in early 1974 when Rathgeb and crew arrived at Concord, the new Kit Car had been tested only once, with promising results, at the Caraway Speedway, an asphalt oval in Asheboro, North Carolina. Dirt tracks were still very much in vogue, and the project car had to also work on dirt to be successful. Unfortunately, Hamilton, the test driver Rathgeb had hired, confessed to him at the end of the test at Caraway, "I've never been on dirt before. You need somebody who can drive on dirt."

"I wish you'd told me that before I hired you," groused Rathgeb, who resolved to take his crew to Concord and find a driver. That crew included Powell, a veteran racer on assignment at Petty Enterprises where the experimental project had been undertaken, and Randy Owens, The King's brother-in-law.

Rathgeb decided to call Harry Hyde, the savvy crew chief running Buddy Baker in Dodge Chargers on the Winston Cup circuit, and tell him of his plight. It didn't take Hyde long to reply: "I'll have a young man up there for you. If you don't like him, call back and let me know."

Hyde, who lived near the Concord track, was confident of his choice; he had watched Ralph Earnhardt's son start in the V-6 class at Concord three years earlier, and then go on to win the overall championships at the Charlotte Fairgrounds and at the outlaw track at Concord. Typical of the times, aspiring drivers were falling off every short-track pit wall without much notice, especially the ones at dirt tracks. That included the lanky, broad-shouldered young man who met Rathgeb at Concord to test the Kit Car.

It didn't take long to realize why Hyde had suggested this particular driver. "He just oozed talent from the minute he got into the car," said Powell, who had worked with Indy 500 winner Parnelli Jones and the previous year's Winston (98) Cup champion, Benny Parsons, as well as with The King. No wonder Earnhardt, although outwardly shy, had let it be known among friends that he was "superior on dirt."

"We got up in the grandstands on top of the track to watch and time him," said Rathgeb. "It was clear to me that this guy was certainly talented and that he was a born driver. The throttle response wasn't harsh and he picked it up early coming out of the corners. You could watch how the car behaved and see he had good responses."

More important to Rathgeb, the young charge was consistent on the stopwatch. "If the times were slow, they were consistently slow," he said. "If they were fast, they were

Looking for a driver for 1979, newcomer Rod Osterlund auditioned Earnhardt (98) at Atlanta's Dixie 500, the next-to-last race of the season. He finished fourth. Marcis left in a dispute after the season, and occasional driver Roland Wlodykz stepped up to team manager. *Bryant McMurray*

consistently fast." That gave the prototype team the feedback it needed regarding the car's responses to various changes made on the chassis, the crucial element of the test. The rookie test driver made precise comments on the car's handling. "The report back as to what the car did was very good," said Rathgeb.

There were two extraordinary moments during the test. One occurred midway in the day when Earnhardt crashed in Turn 1. "Dale got out of the car with a worried look on his face," said Rathgeb. Throughout his career Earnhardt would destroy many cars, especially his own in the coming years during his struggles on short tracks. When the cars belonged to someone else, and the car was regarded as crucial to his ambitions, Earnhardt would become almost sick with panic. This fear about wrecking borrowed cars

came from his earliest days as a driver, when brother-in-law David Oliver loaned him a car to race for the first time at Concord and his stern father had told the Oliver family, "If Dale wrecks it, we aren't going to fix it."

Three years down the road, Dale's wreck during the Kit Car test left him woozy, but not from any physical injury. "He thought we were going to fire him on the spot," said Rathgeb. "I told him, 'Don't worry about it.'" With an anxious Earnhardt helping out—just like he had always done with his father and on his own cars—Powell got the Kit Car repaired and the test resumed that afternoon.

When it was over, another extraordinary moment arrived. Although shy and sometimes choppy with his words, the young driver had resolve and a quiet confidence. Still, Rathgeb was taken by surprise when Earnhardt sat with him on the pit wall following the test and directly asked him for help. "My father died last September," Earnhardt said, "and I don't hardly know what to do with myself."

The original plan had been for Dale to run a second car with his barnstorming father on the dirt-track circuit after he had earned his spurs running locally. He still had his father's Camaros and a ready-made crew in his two brothers, Randy and Danny, but the racing times were changing. NASCAR was beginning to emphasize asphalt short tracks as stepping stones to the superspeedways, and Earnhardt wasn't sure about running outlaw dirt tracks like Concord. His father had won regularly and was a local legend, yet had never made it as a driver in the big NASCAR shows despite occasional appearances on the beach in Daytona and on superspeedways.

Rathgeb was the first person connected with a factory participating in the Grand National that Earnhardt had ever met, much less to whom he had a chance to show his driving ability. For his part, Rathgeb was a bit taken aback by this young man—whom he'd known less than a day—who sought his opinion about such deep concerns.

THE EARLY DAYS

Roland Wlodyka and Earnhardt get the No. 98 car ready for Earnhardt's 1978 run at Atlanta. Dale lived up to the challenge and finished fourth behind Donnie Allison, Richard Petty, and Dave Marcis, who made his last start for the team. With that drive, Earnhardt earned a full-time job for 1979. It was history in the making. *Bryant McMurray*

"He was 22 years old and I was a perfect stranger," said Rathgeb. "But he really got my attention when he asked, 'What should I do?'"

"I told him, 'You're better off going Grand National racing. For a guy like you, that's the only thing to do.'"

It was quite possibly the only objective and trusted opinion Earnhardt ever received on the subject of how to proceed after the man he always turned to for any serious question about racing—his father—was gone. Rathgeb, Earnhardt must have figured, not only was qualified to offer an opinion on his ability, he was also a perfect stranger who didn't have much of an axe to grind.

By contrast, H. A. "Humpy" Wheeler, soon to be promoter at the nearby Charlotte Motor Speedway, needed a local talent like Earnhardt to help fill the grandstands and incessantly pushed the idea of Dale going to the Grand Nationals. Local car and

Earnhardt and Roland Wlodyka stroll through the Osterlund team shop prior to the 1978 Dixie 500. *Bryant McMurray*

engine builders saw the opportunity in Earnhardt to perhaps carry them along into the Grand National ranks. Still others, such as Darrell Waltrip and Harry Gant, soon who competed against him on the short tracks, would pronounce Earnhardt unfit for the Grand Nationals to anyone within earshot, although not necessarily in public.

So Rathgeb's advice would remain crucial to Earnhardt as he began a long, torturous journey into the Winston Cup ranks. It was a journey that would cost him a second divorce and many other personal hardships before he got the break he needed four years later. Earnhardt's ongoing success depended in part upon asking others for their help in the same humbling and direct way he had spoken to Rathgeb. As anyone who ever did this champion a favor was aware, he never forgot somebody who had helped him along the way. So, 20 years after that fateful meeting, Earnhardt let the world know who gave him his first factory ride.

THE
ROD OSTERLUND ERA

1979–1981

FIRST VICTORY

By Al Pearce

Page 24: In a classic depiction of the man's intensity, Earnhardt waits wide-eyed during a pit stop at Richmond as his rivals go by on the track. Earnhardt held on to finish seventh, three laps down, as Darrell Waltrip captured the trophy. *Dick Conway*

Jake Elder couldn't keep the shit-eating grin off his face. He tried—oh, how the man tried—but he couldn't get rid of that knowing smirk, that cat-who-ate-the-canary look. And why not? He'd just seen the future of stock car racing, and its name was Dale Earnhardt. "I told the boy that if he stuck with me," Elder said at the time, "we'd both end up wearing diamonds as big as cow patties."

The date was April 1, 1979. The scene was the Southeastern 500 at the half-mile, obscenely banked Bristol International Raceway in eastern Tennessee. The storied event was Earnhardt's first Grand National victory. If the victory was a coming-of-age party for the 27-year-old rookie driver, it was a moment of unbridled joy for his 43-year-old crew chief.

At the time, Elder was generally recognized as one of NASCAR's best crew chiefs. His résumé included victories with hall of fame legends A. J. Foyt, Mario Andretti, Mark

Donohue, David Pearson, Benny Parsons, and Darrell Waltrip. He didn't open 1979 with Earnhardt, but was summoned early in the season by team owner Rod Osterlund. Osterlund knew he had a thoroughbred in Earnhardt. The problem was that he needed a trainer with the experience and patience of Jake Elder.

Earnhardt had made only seven Winston Cup starts before the moment he later described as the turning point of his career. Those starts were in mid-pack cars, most of them owned by former journeyman drivers desperate to find a young, promising hotshot to keep them in the sport.

In 1975, even with a heavy schedule of NASCAR Late Model Sportsman races, Earnhardt had done a Cup race for Henley Gray at the Charlotte Motor Speedway. He had done two more in 1976; one for Walter Ballard at Charlotte in May, and the other for Johnny Ray at Atlanta in November. He'd teamed again with Gray for the

1977 fall race at Charlotte and had run four races with Will Cronkite in 1978: Charlotte in May, Daytona Beach in July, Talladega in August, and Darlington in September.

The Memorial Day weekend Coca-Cola 600 at Charlotte had made as many off-track headlines as on-track. In a last-minute scramble, promoter Humpy Wheeler had arranged for Earnhardt to drive the Cronkite-owned No. 96 Ford. The car had been prepared with Willy T. Ribbs in mind, but the noted road racer and Indy car star forfeited the opportunity by missing two CMS practice sessions. Worse yet, he

Above: Earnhardt drove a Buick in his first-ever Daytona 500 and was impressive, finishing eighth, a lap down. Ahead of Earnhardt is Joe Millikan (72), one of several challengers for 1979 rookie-of-the-year. Behind Dale are James Hylton and road-racer Al Holbert. *Dick Conway*

The Osterlund team switched to the reliable Chevrolet for the shorter races, including the March stop at Richmond, where Earnhardt finished 13th, 10 laps behind winner Cale Yarborough. This was before power steering, and Earnhardt's head is pressed against the net as he struggles with cornering. *Dick Conway* was arrested for a DWI and driving the wrong way on a one-way street. Earnhardt had qualified 28th and finished 17th, well behind winner Waltrip and lead-lap finishers Donnie Allison, Bobby Allison, Cale Yarborough, Pearson, and Parsons.

Earnhardt also had made one 1978 start for Osterlund, a wealthy California business-man. Nobody realized it at the time—certainly neither the owner nor the driver—but that was the break Earnhardt needed in his climb from weekly dirt track racer to established Grand National driver. That break arrived in almost storybook fashion.

Early in the 1978 season, Earnhardt had made friends with some of the crewmen on Osterlund's team. In time, the crewmen gently persuaded their boss to let them pull a discarded car from the team junkyard and overhaul it for that fall's Late Model Sportsman 300 at CMS. Osterlund relented, but stipulated that the crewmen could work on Earnhardt's car only after business hours. It went without saying that they couldn't use any new parts from Osterlund Racing's inventory.

Earnhardt had stunned Osterlund (and perhaps himself as well) by almost winning the 300-miler. He was leading and seemingly home free when the transmission went bad just 10 laps from the finish. Osterlund was so impressed that he put Earnhardt in one of his Cup cars for the next-to-last race of the season, at Atlanta.

The youngster had made the most of the opportunity, started tenth and finished fourth in the Dixie 500 at Atlanta Motor Speedway. He came in a lap behind established stars Donnie Allison, Richard Petty, and Dave Marcis, his one-off teammate in the Osterlund team's primary car. It was the first of what turned out to be 281 top-five fin-ishes in Earnhardt's 676-start career.

That performance reinforced Osterlund's feeling that this Earnhardt kid—at 27 and hungry as a hound—might be a keeper. His plans for 1979 were to field full-schedule Chevys for Marcis and Earnhardt, the latter a Rookie-of-the-Year contender in the class that included Harry Gant, Terry Labonte, and Joe Millikan.

Marcis balked at the prospect of sharing the team with a rookie. He left to create his own team, and left us to wonder about his possible legacy had he stayed with Osterlund and teamed with Earnhardt for at least the 1979 season. Once Marcis left, Osterlund sim-ply made Earnhardt his primary full-schedule driver. He gave him No. 2, the number Marcis had carried throughout 1978 and would have carried in 1979.

It took only seven races for Earnhardt to prove that Osterlund's faith was well-placed. At Bristol, in only his 16th career start, he started 9th, utterly dominated the 500-lapper, and won the Southeastern 500 over Bobby Allison, Waltrip, Richard Petty, and Parsons. Incidentally, the top-five from that Sunday afternoon would combine to win 465 points races and 19 NASCAR championships)

Did we mention that Earnhardt dominated the race? He led laps 139 and 140 during an exchange of pit stops, then led 255 through 338, and from 474 to the finish at 500. Going into Bristol, he had led only 6 times for 19 laps in his previous 15 Winston Cup starts.

Not surprisingly, his first thoughts were of his father. Ralph Earnhardt, the 1956 NASCAR Sportsman champion, had died of a heart attack in September 1973, well before his hardscrabble son had found his way in the racing world. Dale suffered the aching disappointment that his father didn't live long enough to see what kind of driver/businessman he'd become. He'd often spoken of his father and their special bond, and always in soft and respectful tones.

"I'd like to think my daddy would be proud of me," he'd said that Sunday afternoon in Bristol. "I always wanted to race cars, just like he did. He was my hero and my friend."

Although it's hard to imagine, Harry Gant, 39, also was a "rookie" in the Class of 1979. Earnhardt and Gant were competitors on the old Sportsman tour, so they knew each other well. Dale and Gant discuss matters at Charlotte. *Bryant McMurray*

It became evident in the early laps at Bristol that the fledgling relationship between old chief, Jake Elder, and the young driver was working. Despite qualifying 11th, Earnhardt was a force from the beginning. When Buddy Baker and Cale Yarborough crashed out near halfway, Earnhardt was left with only Waltrip and Bobby Allison as serious challengers.

Richard Petty presses the issue with the rookie late in the World 600 at Charlotte. Petty took the position away from Earnhardt and finished second behind winner Darrell Waltrip. Petty, however, edged Waltrip by 11 points to claim the championship (his seventh). *Dick Conway*

THE ROD OSTERLUND ERA 1979

Other than Donnie Allison's one lap in front, the 500-lapper belonged to Bobby Allison, Baker, Yarborough, Waltrip, and Earnhardt, who led the most laps.

Pit strategy became critical as the race entered its showdown. Waltrip and Earnhardt were so evenly matched that neither could build an appreciable lead on the other. Four times they pitted at the same time, and four times Earnhardt beat Waltrip back to the track, including under the final caution at lap 473. Once, Waltrip took the lead on a restart by faking high and swooping down to the inside, but Earnhardt eventually regained the lead, and covered the spot when Waltrip tried that same maneuver in the final laps.

"He got me with that move one time," Earnhardt said afterward. "But the last time I was in front for a restart, I remembered that he'd gunned it when we were still on the backstretch. So the last time we restarted, I got about halfway down the backstretch and said. 'Well, old Darrell, let's go.' I wasn't taking any chances."

When Waltrip began fading toward the end, Bobby Allison moved to second and took up the chase. It was much too little and much too late, and even the rookie knew it. "I saw Darrell falling back during the last stretch and I wondered why," Earnhardt said. "But pretty soon, he was so far back that I decided not to worry, to drive my own race and quit looking in the mirror. I had to work not to get too overanxious about the whole thing. I was afraid to look for anything except the checkered flag. I kept thinking, 'This time around has got to be it.'"

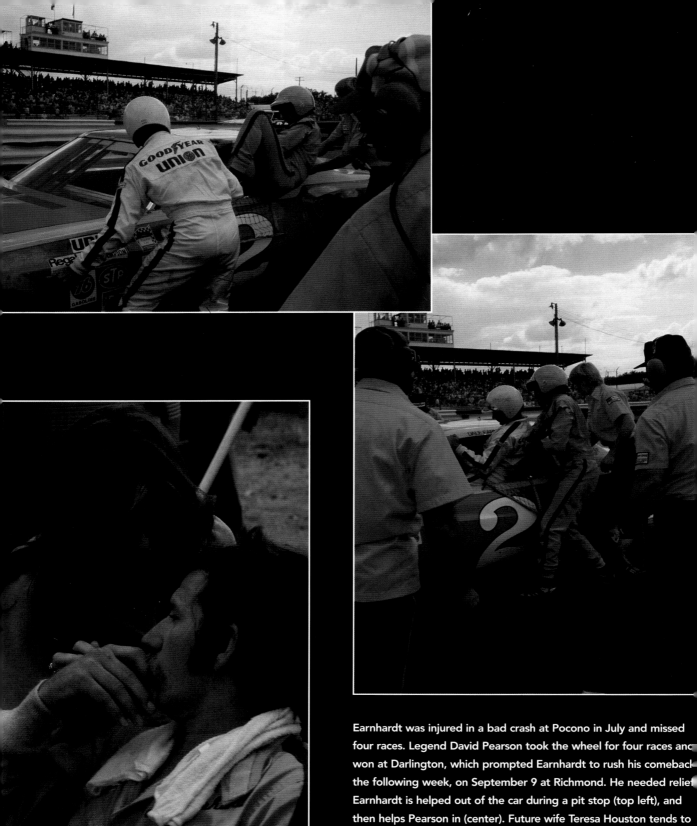

Earnhardt was injured in a bad crash at Pocono in July and missed four races. Legend David Pearson took the wheel for four races and won at Darlington, which prompted Earnhardt to rush his comeback the following week, on September 9 at Richmond. He needed relief Earnhardt is helped out of the car during a pit stop (top left), and then helps Pearson in (center). Future wife Teresa Houston tends to the aching driver in the pits (left). *Dick Conway*

Elder discovered that afternoon what a talent he had under his care, And he knew from experience. He'd been crew chief when Pearson won the 1968 and 1969 NASCAR championships for Holman-Moody. He'd helped Mario Andretti win the Daytona 500. He'd also taken Waltrip from a brash, cocky driver with enormous potential to a brash, cocky driver with victory upon victory.

Earnhardt (2), Richard Petty (43), and Benny Parsons (27) go three-wide past the flagstand in the October race at Rockingham. Although Earnhardt became known as an impetuous charger, the veterans had full trust in the talented rookie. *Bryant McMurray*

"I hate to tell you this because Darrell Waltrip's a close and good friend of mine," Elder said. "But I think this boy has more potential than Darrell. It took Darrell about a year and a half to learn to run with the big boys, but Dale's doing it quicker. The big boys are amazed that he drives so deep into the corners. But that's because he's used to those light Late Model Sportsman cars, those dirt-track cars. I'm telling you, Dale will get even sharper as the year goes on. Right now, I'm just talking to him like he's my son. I watch and worry about him every lap he's out there."

That was appropriate since Elder had known Ralph Earnhardt, watched him win countless races on obscure dirt tracks in the Carolinas in the 1950s and 1960s, and had marveled at his natural talent and legendary determination. "Dale's daddy was a helluva driver," Elder said. "Dale's got it in his blood, too. I could tell that the first time I saw him. He's going to win more. He's going to win on superspeedways and short tracks; there's no kind of track he can't drive. There's no doubt he's a race car driver.

"He'll make a lot of people's eyes bug out. He's sharp and he's going to get sharper; this is only a start for him. I don't have nothing to prove because I've won with every driver I've ever had. But this win today is the biggest in my whole career. I got more satisfaction out of seeing Dale come across that line than any race I can ever remember. He's young and he's good, so if he doesn't get hurt, he's got 10 or 12 years as a top driver."

The race exhausted Waltrip, who seemed to let Allison through for second in the final laps. Early in the season Waltrie said a rookie might win a race, but it might just be a fluke. After the 500, he quickly noted that Earnhardt's victory definitely was not a fluke. "He was the only driver I had to beat all day and I couldn't do it," Waltrie said. "When I was in front of him, he couldn't get by. And when he was in front of me, I couldn't get by. Give him credit, he ran good… really good."

It was hard to tell whether Earnhardt was surprised at winning so quickly or disap-

Above: Re-armed and ready in 1980, Earnhardt and the Rod Osterlund team ran fourth in the Daytona 500 and began the season with six top-fives in a row—a resounding opening to a championship season. The team ran Oldsmobiles on the big tracks and Chevrolets elsewhere. *Bryant McMurray*

Left: Earnhardt earned $50,000 for winning the second running of the Busch Clash at Daytona. The special event matched the previous year's pole-winners against one another. TV commentator and longtime family acquaintance Ned Jarrett interviews Dale in victory lane. *Bryant McMurray*

pointed at not winning sooner. Some of both, most NASCAR watchers suspected at the time. After all, he was the son of the man they called "Ironheart" in grudging admiration of his will to succeed. After the race, the man who would come to be known as "The Intimidator" seemed impressed with himself.

"I'll probably believe it in the morning," he said in victory lane, his unassuming yellow driving suit hardly dampened. "This is a bigger thrill than my first-ever victory. This is in the big leagues, against the best caliber of drivers. It wasn't on some dirt track back home."

He displayed his developing sense of humor by crediting some of NASCAR's biggest stars for helping him along the way. "I've received a lot of help from Bobby Allison and Richard Petty, and a lot of the guys who've been in Grand National," he said. "I sure want to thank them for taking time to talk with me and teach me things. Thing of it is," he said with a wry grin, "I kinda wonder if they'll hush up now."

Earnhardt awaits the call to start engines at Richmond in February. Dale started 13th and finished 5th in the season's first short-track event, three laps behind winner Darrell Waltrip, with Bobby Allison in 2nd. *Dick Conway*

Earnhardt started fourth (right) in the World 600 at Charlotte in May and was in or around the lead past the halfway point. A crash, however, flattened the side of the No. 2 car (below), and Dale struggled to the finish line in 20th place, 33 laps down. *Dick Conway*

Earnhardt and Darrell Waltrip (88) tear through the turns at Charlotte. Waltrip, in his last season with DiGard, led the most laps but finished second, when Benny Parsons took the lead with two laps to go. The race included a one-hour red flag and covered more than six hours of clock time. *Dick Conway*

The Osterlund team commences its celebration as the car heads for victory lane at Martinsville in September. This was the fourth of Earnhardt's five victories in 1980, and he followed up with another trophy the next week at Charlotte. *Dick Conway*

A look inside the Osterlund Racing shop shows one of each car: a Chevrolet in the foreground and an Oldsmobile in back. Osterlund, a land developer from California, had assembled a championship team in just two years. *Bryant McMurray*

THE ROD OSTERLUND ERA 1980

Earnhardt sits at the arm of king-maker Junior Johnson, three-time champion car owner and a man of untold influence in NASCAR. Johnson took a liking to the young driver and was instrumental in the development of Earnhardt's career over the next few years. *Bryant McMurray*

Earnhardt's passions away from the track were bird hunting and fishing, but he took a crack at golf during a celebrity tournament at Rockingham. Here, he shows a decidedly amateur swing from the tee. *Bryant McMurray*

Earnhardt enjoyed sports other than racing. He was an avid baseball fan, especially of the Atlanta Braves, and became friends with longtime Braves manager Bobby Cox and several players. Earnhardt also played in a charity basketball game at Daytona Beach in 1981. *Brian Cleary*

With Earnhardt and the team closing in on the championship, the fall victory at Charlotte was especially sweet. The win gave Earnhardt a 115-point lead over three-time champ Cale Yarborough, but he had a fight to the finish at Ontario, California, and beat Cale by just 19 points, the second-closest points race in history up to that time. *Bryant McMurray*

Decked out in new Wrangler colors, the Osterlund crew pushes its car from inspection to the qualifying line at Daytona in February 1981, as Earnhardt commenced the most turbulent season of his career. He qualified seventh and finished fifth in the 500. *Dick Conway*

Earnhardt was considerably more flamboyant in his early years and frequently wore a Richard Petty-style cowboy hat. In the garage at Daytona, he gets the numbers from crew chief Doug Richert (left). *Dick Conway*

Caution came out early in the 1981 Daytona 500, with Earnhardt and Bobby Allison (28) contending for the lead. Neil Bonnett (21) is behind Allison, while Benny Parsons (15) trails Earnhardt. Allison finished second to Richard Petty. *Dick Conway*

The principals in Earnhardt's tenure with Osterlund were team manager Roland Wlodyka (left) and, of course, owner Rod Osterlund. Visionary but mercurial, Osterlund suddenly and without warning cashed out of the game at midyear, and left Dale stranded. *Bryant McMurray*

Clean-cut and somewhat fresh-faced, Earnhardt poses on pit road at Darlington in March 1981. Darlington still relied on its infamous old guardrail, which shows a battering and was the cause of the cars' traditional "Darlington stripes." *Dick Conway*

THE ROD OSTERLUND ERA 1981

Morgan Shepherd (5) and Richard Petty (43) force Earnhardt to the outside at Martinsville, as Terry Labonte (44) awaits his chance. Shepherd, a rookie in 1981, won for the first time in this race. *Dick Conway*

A famous early photo of Earnhardt taken by photographer Don Hunter stares down from a promotional billboard at Charlotte Motor Speedway in May 1981. As a local hero and defending Winston Cup champion, Earnhardt had become a regional icon. *Dick Conway*

Earnhardt fights through a crowd at Michigan in August, his first race with Childress. Ricky Rudd (88) is inside, with Darrell Waltrip (11) on the outside and Benny Parsons following just behind. Dale finished ninth, on the lead lap, in a race won by Richard Petty. *Bryant McMurray*

When Rod Osterlund sold his team to J. D. Stacy at mid-season 1981, Earnhardt grew uncomfortable and left to join Richard Childress in a deal brokered by Junior Johnson. An offer of $75,000 in Wrangler sponsorship money persuaded Childress to quit driving and yield the wheel and leave the driving to Earnhardt. *Bryant McMurray*

THE
BUD MOORE ERA

1982–1983

Page 46: Earnhardt and Bud Moore (right) enjoy one of their few bright spots of 1982—victory lane at Darlington in April. It was Earnhardt's first win of the season and the seventh of his career. Unfortunately it was also the only victory in a frustrating year. *Bryant McMurray*

Page 47: Despite a blown engine at Daytona, the 1982 season did not begin badly, with top-fives in three of the first four events: Riverside (fourth), Richmond (fourth and seen here), and Bristol (second). Earnhardt finished third in laps led that year, but couldn't seem to finish and ended up 12th in points. *Dick Conway*

It's a little-remembered fact that Earnhardt won the first race in NASCAR's reformed Sportsman Series, the Goody's 300, at Daytona in February 1982. The new circuit was not yet called the Busch Series. *Bryant McMurray*

A Tough Day at Darlington

By David Green

Dale Earnhardt and the Bud Moore Engineering team rolled into Darlington Raceway for the Rebel 500, the sixth race of the 1982 season, determined to score their first victory of the year.

Earnhardt qualified fifth with the Bud Moore Thunderbird, which had an engine and handling package capable of running up front. The team's chances of winning the 500-mile race depended on 16 small, but important, parts inside the engine of the No. 15 Wrangler-sponsored Thunderbird. Valve springs were the Achilles' heel of the handful of NASCAR Ford teams. The bright blue-and-yellow car Earnhardt drove was plenty competitive, but engine failures had thwarted his best chances to win.

A strategic error knocked Earnhardt out of the Daytona 500. The team cut Earnhardt a half-lap short on fuel, and a piston burned when the engine leaned out as it sought for gasoline. He was leading at the time. Three races later, at Atlanta International Raceway, Earnhardt won the pole and was out front when the engine's valvetrain failed.

The car was potent. He could lead whenever he wanted to. Leading made Earnhardt happy, but winning made him much happier.

The members of Moore's veteran crew loved Earnhardt. He was one of the boys. Whenever they went testing or to a race, Dale was all business. Off the clock, Earnhardt showed respect for Moore's crew. He flew to and from the tracks aboard the same twin-engine King Air that carried the crew to the distant stops on the Winston Cup tour. On race weekends, he always went out to dinner with them. In rare free moments, he went hunting with rear tire changer Harold Stott and gasman Phil Thomas. The efforts he made to bond with them, and the obvious intensity, about his job in the cockpit of the No. 15 car, made for a solid driver-team combination. Earnhardt made himself at home in this secondary family, and was certain things would look up again after a frustrating 1981.

Success had come relatively quickly for Earnhardt as a Winston Cup driver. He tested the waters of the big leagues by competing in nine races over a four-year period from 1975 to 1978; then, at 27, he joined forces with California businessman Rod Osterlund, who was starting a NASCAR race team of his own. Earnhardt got his first victory early in the 1979 season, at Bristol, and even though he did not add a second victory, he won Rookie-of-the-Year honors over fellow first-year drivers Terry Labonte and Harry Gant. Earnhardt clearly established himself as a driver and contender among Richard Petty, David Pearson, Cale Yarborough, and rising superstar Darrell Waltrip. The next year, Earnhardt won five races and

Earnhardt, with the blessing of Richard Childress, joined Bud Moore's established No. 15 team for 1982 and set out to win a championship. Although the results, mixed at first, only grew worse. In the end, Earnhardt tallied 17 DNFs, and all but three of them mechanical. Here, Ricky Rudd, now driving Childress' No. 3, gives chase at Atlanta in late March. *Bryant McMurray*

captured the 1980 Winston Cup. It was the first time any driver had won rookie and championship titles in back-to-back seasons.

Despite a long-term contract and the addition of Wrangler Jeans as sponsor, the combination of Earnhardt and Osterlund would not last long. Midway through the 1981 season, a financially strapped Osterlund sold the operation and Earnhardt left the team after four races under the new owner, J. D. Stacy. He finished the season with the team of journeyman racer Richard Childress, who had surrendered the steering wheel to become a full-time team owner. Great things were in store for Earnhardt and Childress, but none of them would happen in 1981: two fourth-place finishes were the best the new combination could produce. Even when those races were combined with Earnhardt's performance in the Osterlund/Stacy cars—two runner-up finishes were his best showings—the driver who had been the sensation of 1979 and 1980 went winless in his third season.

Down on his luck but not completely out of it, Earnhardt received an offer to drive for one of NASCAR's established teams at the end of 1981. The offer came from Bud Moore, whose Spartanburg, South Carolina-based team had won championships in 1962 and 1963 with the late Joe Weatherly driving. More recently, Moore had fielded top-drawer entries for Bobby Allison and Benny Parsons. In three of the best seasons of his illustrious career, Allison was consistently in the hunt for the Winston Cup championship (second in 1978, third in 1979, and eighth in 1980) and won 14 races, including the 1978 Daytona 500. He left Moore's team to drive for Harry Ranier in 1981, and Moore, with Parsons driving, saw his cars roar to three more victories.

Next in the all-star parade of drivers to wheel Moore's machines was Earnhardt.

Just about the only downside of the deal was Moore's relationship with Ford Motor Company. Even though his first race car was a pink 1956 Ford, the identity Earnhardt would develop as one of Chevrolet's most famous representatives was not merely a public relations campaign: Earnhardt really favored Chevys. Although he was even more fond of winning. Ford had been a powerhouse in racing. Earnhardt's father, Ralph, had made his Winston Cup debut in 1957 in a factory-sponsored Ford entry. Now, Ford Motor Company was planning to end a decade-long absence from NASCAR racing, and Moore's team figured prominently in the plans. Earnhardt, everyone figured, was just the driver they needed.

Although he had one champion's trophy already, the 30-year-old, bushy-haired, mustachioed Earnhardt was still perfecting his trade. Years later, Earnhardt would say, "Bud Moore taught me how to win races." Moore downplayed the compliment and admitted that he and Earnhardt talked at length about things such as reading changes in the track and translating them into effective adjustments, either in the car's set-up or in the line Earnhardt was using to get around the track. Moore also helped the aggressive Earnhardt refine his driving tactics. He showed Earnhardt the advantage of thinking

Earnhardt and Richard Petty hug the wall at Darlington in order to pass the lapped car of J. D. McDuffie (70), one of the sport's most determined pluggers. Earnhardt led 182 of the race's 367 laps and was one of only 17 on the lead lap at the finish. *Bryant McMurray*

Earnhardt, psyched for competition, gives his window net a last-minute tug as he readies for the start at Richmond in September. Dale started sixth in this race (he won only one pole all year), but his engine quit after 158 laps. *Dick Conway*

The Bud Moore crew pits Earnhardt's car at Richmond, as Richard Petty steams back to action. Few present-day fans remember the sometimes primitive conditions under which the Winston Cup tour raced in those times: check the flagstand and grandstands in the background. *Dick Conway*

ahead, planning how he could best overtake other competitors with a minimum loss of his own rhythm and momentum.

Moore later said Earnhardt was a naturally gifted driver who needed little guidance. "One thing about him, he wanted to be out front, and he was gonna be out front if the car held up," Moore said. "He had a good feel of a race car, and I'd say, 'What do you think we need to do?' and he used to tell me, 'You fix it, I'll drive it.' And that's what he did. We'd get to the race track and practice and talk about this and that, and he'd say, 'You think that's what to do, you do it.' He'd find a way around the race track. Some way, somehow, he'd find a way to outrun you."

In his first five races in Moore's car, Earnhardt lived up to the most optimistic expectations and proved to be just the right man for the job. Now, if only the team could supply engines that would stand up to Earnhardt's demands.

As race day dawned at Darlington, Earnhardt was in character. His concentration focused on the mission at hand, but the intensity was belied by low-key emotions. There was no unusual urgency for the veteran crew. The best possible preparations had been made; Moore had arrived early to remove the valve covers and replace all the valve

Earnhardt chases Ricky Rudd (3) into the first turn at the start of the fall 1982 race at Rockingham. Earnhardt fell out with a broken engine 40 laps from the finish, amid a streak of eight consecutive DNFs to close out the season. *Bryant McMurray*

springs with brand-new parts. The race got under way with front-row starters Buddy Baker and Darrell Waltrip taking turns leading the first two laps. Then Neil Bonnett took command to pace the third and fourth laps. At that point, Earnhardt surged to the front for the first time. He held the lead for seven laps before Bonnett passed him. It was clear Earnhardt was one of the race favorites, and he would never be far from the front throughout the highly competitive race.

With 90 laps to go in the 367-lap chase, Earnhardt, who had already paced the race 8 times for 81 laps, took command from Benny Parsons and set sail. Moore kept a close eye on his stopwatch and radioed Earnhardt, "Slow her down, take her easy. You know those valve springs ain't gonna last." Earnhardt pedaled the Thunderbird a bit, but the next thing Moore knew, his driver's lap times were a little quicker, first a tenth of a second, then another tenth. Moore keyed his radio again. "Man, take it easy, you're still out-running everybody else!" He was torn between elation at the way Earnhardt was whipping the field and anxiety over how long the whipping was going to last.

As the race neared its conclusion, Cale Yarborough, a native of nearby Sardis and a proven master of the treacherous, irregular-shaped Darlington oval, moved his Chevy in on Earnhardt's rear bumper. That gave Earnhardt and Moore something to worry about besides valve springs. After Yarborough put his car ahead as the 355th lap was complet-ed, Earnhardt regained command for the last time. The engine went the distance and Earnhardt led Yarborough across the finish line by a scant 0.023 second.

The checkered flag flashed and cheers erupted from underneath the roof of the old track's covered grandstand as Earnhardt and Yarborough rumbled under deceleration toward the first turn. In the pits, Moore's face lit up with a grin. Stott, Thomas, Doug Williams, Ray

Identified with Chevrolet for most of his career, Earnhardt spent two seasons in Bud Moore's Fords. The new, slick Thunderbird replaced the boxier, old model in 1983, but teething trouble with the Ford small-block persisted, and Dale accumulated DNFs throughout the season—including eight in the season's first nine races. *Dick Conway*

Harris, and other crewmembers exchanged congratulations in a victory celebration that Stott remembers as the sweetest of the 40 or so that he took part.

"We had good stops that day, naturally," recalled Stott. "But Dale won the race for us. He drove and drove hard. As tough as Darlington is, and to beat somebody like Cale, it was something."

It was the third Darlington victory for Moore, and the first of nine wins Earnhardt would score at the tough old track. Only David Pearson (10 victories) won more at Darlington. Moore was optimistic that it signaled an end to the engine problems that had revealed themselves in the first five races of the campaign, but that optimism would prove false. Earnhardt was the dominant driver for the next two seasons as far as laps led, but it was Darrell Waltrip in 1982 and Bobby Allison in 1983 who celebrated championship titles.

The Darlington victory would be the only win of the 1982 season. Earnhardt would score two more wins in Moore's Fords in 1983. He stopped a Waltrip win streak at Waltrip's home track in Nashville and claimed his first of ten wins at massive Talladega. That wasn't good enough for Earnhardt, who was impatient with Ford's efforts to place reliable engine components at his disposal.

"I think Dale Earnhardt would have still been driving for me if we'd had the engines

THE BUD MOORE ERA 1983

Earnhardt and Darrell Waltrip always seemed to be at war, and the tight half-mile at Martinsville guaranteed hand-to-hand combat. Waltrip won the April race, and Earnhardt and another fierce rival, Geoff Bodine, crashed out on the 351st lap. *Dick Conway*

Earnhardt works to hold off Bill Elliott at Charlotte in May. Throughout his career, Earnhardt considered Charlotte his home track, as one of his favorites. *Bryant McMurray*

that would have stood Dale Earnhardt's foot," Moore said. "Of all the races we run in 1982 and 1983, I don't know of a one we didn't lead and wasn't out front when the engine let go."

In 1984, Earnhardt rejoined the Childress team that finished with in the winless 1981 season. Ricky Rudd, who had gotten the first two victories for Childress' famous No. 3 in 1983, went to Moore's team for a successful four-year stint.

Old and New. The differences between the 1982 Thunderbird (above) and the 1983 model (right) were obvious. The new 'Bird was low-slung and slick, and the older car was big and boxy—a true "stock" car. The new model also heralded the modern era of aerodynamics in NASCAR. *Bryant McMurray*

Moore knew that Earnhardt and Childress had hit it off pretty well, despite the unimpressive statistics of their half-season together in 1981. He certainly was not surprised by the incredible success Earnhardt and Childress enjoyed after they reunited.

"It's hard to say what makes a special driver such as Earnhardt," Moore said. "There's a lot of difference in a race driver that's out there running and one that wants to win. The one that wants to win is gonna win, eventually. You take somebody like Dale Earnhardt, Bobby Allison, Buddy Baker, and a few others. That desire to win is what really pushes 'em."

The Bud Moore crew, considered one of the best of its time, goes to work on Earnhardt's car during caution stops at Charlotte in May 1983. Moore began to solve mechanical problems by late spring, with "only" five more DNFs the rest of the way. *Bryant McMurray*

Earnhardt tows Darrell Waltrip (11) and Tim Richmond (27) toward the front at Michigan in August. Dale finished seventh, on the lead lap, and Waltrip finished second behind winner Cale Yarborough. *Bryant McMurray*

Lower right: Earnhardt also had Wrangler support
in the fledgling Busch Grand National Series, successor to the old Sportsman circuit. Earnhardt paced a Wrangler *Oldsmobile* in the GN preliminary at Charlotte, with Charlie Luck just behind. *Dick Conway*

Parallel Universe. Ricky Rudd continued to stabilize the Richard Childress team during Earnhardt's term with Bud Moore. The teams swapped back in 1984, with both Rudd and Earnhardt racing under the Wrangler banner. *Dick Conway*

THE
KIRK SHELMERDINE ERA

1984–1992

THE LOSING STREAK BEGINS

By Jonathan Ingram

At the 1986 Daytona 500, Dale Earnhardt surely had the car, talent, and strategy to win stock car racing's biggest event. The slightest of errors launched one of motor racing's best known losing streaks. In the ensuing years, Earnhardt often came close but had trouble winning the Daytona 500. Typical of his determination, his initial painful loss at Daytona did not deter Earnhardt from the goal of winning the Winston Cup at season's end, his first with Richard Childress Racing.

The Childress team arrived at Daytona Beach in February of 1986 after they accomplished some of the goals established when Earnhardt and Ricky Rudd had traded places two years earlier. In 1984, the Virginia driver had moved to the Fords of Bud Moore, and Earnhardt switched from Moore's squad to the Childress team. Both drivers retained Wrangler Jeans sponsorship.

The first goal for Childress after the swap was to re-establish Earnhardt as a winner. Earnhardt had won only three races since his 1980 title season with Rod Osterlund's team, and sponsor Wrangler was antsy enough to add Rudd to its driver line-up. Meanwhile, the Childress team had made the transition to winning status with its first trip to victory lane with Rudd at Riverside, California, in 1983.

"When Dale came over to Richard Childress in 1984, he had lost his confidence," said Lou LaRosa, the engine builder for Childress. A lifelong racer from Brooklyn, LaRosa certainly knew Earnhardt well enough to make such a judgment. He had built the Chevy V-8s that the North Carolinian had used to stun the racing world in 1980 when he became the first driver to win the Winston Cup in his second season. An unexpected change came when businessman Osterlund sold his team to coal miner J. D. Stacy midway through the 1981 season. Earnhardt abruptly left after just four races with Stacy and was replaced by Tim Richmond. "Stacy told Dale that he could find a driver anywhere," said LaRosa. "I think

Earnhardt and old buddy Neil Bonnett discuss a private matter at Daytona in one of the few secluded spots available in those days—between the haulers. Bonnett had just begun the first year of a disappointing two-year stand with Junior Johnson. *Dick Conway*

Darrell Waltrip (11) leads Tim Richmond (red car) and Cale Yarborough (29) out of the pits at Darlington in April, while Bill Elliott (9), Terry Labonte (44), Earnhardt, and Richard Petty complete their stops. Waltrip won the race, and Earnhardt finished fifth, a lap down. *Dick Conway*

that shook him up and he was beginning to believe it."

Two victories with Childress in the 1984 season and four short-track wins during the 1985 campaign restored Earnhardt's confidence. Although when Bill Elliott drove to a record 11 superspeedway victories during that same 1985 season—and the Chevy engines began popping like corn due to a poor parts supply line from General Motors—Earnhardt still faced stiff challenges to his goal of winning the championship. Fortunately, General Motors responded with a Monte Carlo SS for the 1986 season with a sloped rear window, that fed air to the spoiler much like the Ford Thunderbird of Elliott.

A crewman ties up loose ends for Earnhardt before the start of the race at Charlotte in May, as wife Teresa looks on. The older-style Childress No. 3 was still used in 1984; the change to the more-famous, rounded "3" was made the next season. *Dick Conway*

"The new cars don't get bogged down," said Childress. "We can use a narrower power band and get back up to speed quicker in the corners." Earnhardt, who had beaten Elliott earlier in the Busch Clash, followed up with a victory in the second Twin 125-mile qualifying race. "When Dale won the 125-mile race, it wasn't even a struggle," said LaRosa. "You could tell by the look on his face."

"When Chevy came out with the

Earnhardt at Charlotte in Wrangler livery. Although the Earnhardt persona was fully realized with GM's "Man in Black" colors, Wrangler's "One Tough Customer" label certainly helped hatch the legend. *Dick Conway*

fastback, the Chevy teams could lay down their rear spoilers just like the Fords," continued LaRosa. "We were fast right off the bat and I knew we were on to something. People were saying I must have come up with a lot more horsepower, and back then we weren't running restrictor plates. The difference was the aerodynamics."

Earnhardt also won the 300-mile Busch Series race on Saturday that gave him a clean sweep of Speed Weeks headed into the final day. After starting third in the 500 behind the pole-winning Ford of Elliott and Geoff Bodine's Hendrick Motorsports Chevy, Earnhardt again found plenty of speed in his Wrangler Monte Carlo. For his part, Elliott

Earnhardt tracks down Geoff Bodine (5) at Charlotte in May 1984, with Buddy Baker (21) on the outside. Dale finished second to Bobby Allison, which launched a streak of 11 top-10 finishes. *Dick Conway*

fell a lap down when he suffered damage to his Ford in a multi-car accident that left only five cars on the lead lap when the green waved with 75 laps remaining.

Three laps later, a fateful caution fell for Grant Adcox's spin. It presented the Childress team an opportunity to add more fuel under a yellow. Then the final stop could be made half the distance from the finish, or 35 laps from the checkered flag, to guarantee

Earnhardt and crew finally broke through to victory in July at Talladega. It was Earnhardt's second victory at the monster track, and his first win with car owner Richard Childress. RC is in the background, to the right of big, bearded Chocolate Myers. *Bryant McMurray*

Earnhardt, a legend in the making, duels with all-time legend Richard Petty at Richmond in September. Petty won his 200th race in 1984. Although it was his last trip to victory lane, it took The King another eight years to bow out. Both cars show short-track battle scars. *Dick Conway*

Earnhardt and Ricky Rudd carried the same sponsor colors through 1984 as part of the transaction that sent Rudd to Bud Moore and Earnhardt to Richard Childress. Rudd is in Moore's Ford. Earnhardt is in the RCR Chevrolet. *Dick Conway*

Earnhardt would make it, even under a sustained green. A disagreement broke out in the pit. LaRosa told crew chief Kirk Shelmerdine that Earnhardt needed to come in and get more fuel.

"Track position is pretty important right now, too," replied Shelmerdine.

From third place, Terry Labonte and Billy Hagan's team elected to give up track position and come in for fuel during the yellow that lasted only three laps. It proved to be a mistake, one that Labonte would look back on with some regret after 24 winless years in

The *real* No. 3 sits on jacks next to an artist's depiction of the car on the side of the Childress team's hauler. Although the rendering and the real car have different in paint schemes, the design on the car is what was run all year. *Dick Conway*

Earnhardt takes care of business with owner Richard Childress (left) and crewman Will Lind during a break at Richmond in September 1984. The three men appear to be relaxed, confident, and comfortable with one another. *Dick Conway*

the 500. "Where I lost the advantage was by being caught at the end of the field (after leaving the pits) on the final restart," he said.

Shelmerdine was right about track position. Once back under the green, Bodine, whose Chevy was directed by Gary Nelson, and Earnhardt exchanged the lead twice in Turn 3, but the second-placed Earnhardt radioed to the pits that he had Bodine covered. "I'm just cruisin'," said Earnhardt.

Earnhardt had the advantage of fresher left side tires because Shelmerdine had elected to change four during a quick entry to the pit lane under the caution for the multi-car accident, while Nelson had put just two right-side Goodyears on for Bodine. Now with a faster Chevy, Shelmerdine was left with only two concerns. Would Bodine change four tires on his last stop? Would both cars be able to make the finish on fuel?

Still holding what looked like nothing but aces, Shelmerdine watched as Bodine came down pit road with 41 laps to go, took on two tires plus fuel, and returned to the track. That meant Earnhardt could change just two tires and still have fresher inside rubber than his adversary. By pitting a lap later, he would also very likely get to the finish on fuel. No one really

Terry Labonte (44) controls the inside against Earnhardt heading into the third turn at the old Richmond Fairgrounds half-mile. Labonte, two-time winner in 1984, went on to win the season championship for owner Billy Hagan and Piedmont Airlines (which later became USAirways). *Dick Conway*

Ricky Rudd (15) and Earnhardt go door-to-door at Richmond in February 1985, with Earnhardt rolling to the first of his four 1985 victories. *Dick Conway*

Neil Bonnett (12) leaves the groove as his car smokes out at Richmond. Earnhardt trails Geoff Bodine (5) through the fast lane on the greasy old half-mile. Bonnett, Earnhardt's closest friend and Darrell Waltrip's teammate, was driving a second car for Junior Johnson in 1985. *Dick Conway*

Earnhardt and crew do some on-the-spot troubleshooting during practice. Note the sparse interior of the car. Many of today's safety improvements, driver comforts, and TV gadgets were still a long way in the future. *Dick Conway*

Earnhardt, owner Richard Childress, and wife Teresa celebrate victory in what was then called the Miller 400 at Richmond. Childress sports the sponsor's cap. The Richmond race at the time was a week after the Daytona 500, accounting for the tanned faces. *Dick Conway*

knew, however, since no team had run an entire green flag segment as they headed into the final stops.

Earnhardt roared onto the pit road where there was no speed limit with 40 laps remaining. But where Bodine whistled down pit road and Nelson's crew cracked off a quick stop, Earnhardt over-cooked his braking and slid through his pit stall. A hectic 19 seconds later, the Wrangler Chevy returned to the track—trailing Bodine by five seconds.

Richard Childress (left), Earnhardt, crew chief Kirk Shelmerdine (third from left), and the rest of the gang pose with the car after winning the 1985 Unocal Pit Crew Competition at Rockingham. The Childress crew set the standard for pit work in the late 1980s.
Dick Conway

Within 14 laps, however, Earnhardt had reeled in the Levi Garrett Chevy, and demonstrated that he indeed had legs on the other Monte Carlo, especially with fresh left-side rubber.

A traditional slingshot pass for the victory loomed for Earnhardt, who continued to wear out Bodine's older tires by hectoring his rear bumper. "I slowed down two or three seconds per lap," said Bodine, "because he was working my car extremely hard in the turns." Although all was not well in the Childress pits, where anxiety over fuel began to loom. Had they gotten enough fuel in the car during the riotous drill on his last stop?

Earnhardt was still harassing Bodine's rear bumper when he ran out of fuel with three laps remaining. "What are we going to do?" shouted Childress, who grabbed a can of ether in case Earnhardt stalled. When the conked-out car floated into the pits, the team owner not only went over the wall, he went overboard when spraying the ether under the cowling to help the engine re-fire.

Earnhardt seeks advice from veteran crew chief Harry Hyde, then with Geoff Bodine. Hyde helped find what became the Hendrick Motorsports powerhouse. In 1985, with one team and one driver, the Hendrick effort was still called "All-Star Racing." *Dick Conway*

The Childress crew checks the fuel cell and connections on the No. 3 in the old garages at Charlotte in May. Parked next to Earnhardt's Wrangler car is the Miller car of Bobby Allison, a fierce rival of Earnhardt—and just about everyone else. *Dick Conway*

The garage was a decidedly more relaxed place in 1985. Leonard Wood (in chair), younger of the legendary Wood Brothers (car owners for Kyle Petty that year), chats with an unidentified man, as Lake Speed (background) reads a racing paper. Earnhardt's unmanned car sits down the row. *Dick Conway*

Earnhardt leads a close battle into Turn 1 at Rockingham. It's hard to make out the second-place car, but that's Bill Elliott in the background. Earnhardt finished eighth in the fall race at The Rock and wasn't yet in championship contention. The top stars at that time were Elliott and Darrell Waltrip. *Bryant McMurray*

The engine coughed, fired, and Earnhardt rolled away, but he never got beyond the apron in Turn 1. The ether had caused enough detonation to destroy the engine. Instead of finishing fourth and last on the lead lap, Earnhardt stewed while the Wrangler Chevy sat on the apron and budding rival Bodine won the Daytona 500, 11 seconds ahead of Labonte. Old rival Elliott pushed Earnhardt's Monte Carlo back to the pits on the cool-down lap.

Earnhardt, his friends often pointed out, didn't love winning as much as he hated losing. Like the rest of his team, he took the painful loss in stride. "If we had pitted on that last caution, we might have been able to stretch it to the finish," he said. "But we didn't pit, and Bodine didn't pit either. He made it, and we didn't."

In private, it was not an easy episode for the Childress team. "You only get so many chances to win the Daytona 500. Your number only comes up every so often," said LaRosa, who left the

As became customary over the years, Earnhardt won everything in sight during February Speed Weeks—everything, that is, except the Daytona 500. In 1986, he hoisted the Busch Clash trophy and also won the Twin qualifier. *Bryant McMurray*

the General Motors cars, such as Earnhardt's Chevrolets, up to par with the sleek Fords, NASCAR allowed a sloped rear glass "fastback" shape in 1986. Earnhardt paces the new-look Chevy at Daytona. *Dick Conway*

track still convinced the team should have brought Earnhardt in under the last yellow. "How can you lose track position if you're the fastest car on the track?" he wondered.

Ultimately, Earnhardt responded with what would become a trademark of his championship seasons with Childress. He didn't dwell on the problems of the Daytona 500 and focused on the points race. Besides, the team now knew it had a Chevy that could run with the Fords on the superspeedways and a driver who could be top gun on the short tracks.

Earnhardt took the points lead with a second-place finish at Talladega later that spring. Despite an all-out chase by Darrell Waltrip and Tim Richmond, the Childress team clinched its first championship prior to the Riverside finale with a victory in Atlanta. It was the second title for Earnhardt, who would not allow annual losses in the Daytona 500 to get in the way of five more Winston Cup championships.

Earnhardt chases Geoff Bodine (5) and Tim Richmond (25) down the backstretch in the 1986 Daytona 500. Bodine won the race when Earnhardt ran out of gas three laps from the finish, a failure Earnhardt called one of his most bitter disappointments. *Dick Conway*

Florida sunshine lights a pre-restrictor plate crowd shot at Daytona. The pack features a "who's who" of the era, including Buddy Baker (88), Geoff Bodine (5), Earnhardt, Benny Parsons (55), and Tim Richmond (25). *Dick Conway*

Earnhardt addresses a well-attended press conference at Rockingham in March. Conducting the Q&A is legendary North Carolina broadcaster Charlie Harville, who would go on to interview three generations of racing Earnhardts. *Dick Conway*

Earnhardt, shoulders square and eyes on the prize, wears his familiar Wrangler uniform, but sports a GM Goodwrench cap. Goodwrench, an associate sponsor in 1986, announced later in the year that it would become the primary sponsor on the No. 3 car. *Dick Conway*

Almost forgotten in Busch Series lore were the two races at the Road Atlanta course in 1986 and 1987—the first ever Busch road races. Terry Labonte (44) leads this group in the 1986 installment, with Earnhardt fourth in line in the black No. 8. Earnhardt finished third. *Dick Conway*

The 1986 season's top contenders, Darrell Waltrip and Earnhardt, talk it over at midseason. Waltrip liked to rattle his rivals with words, but Earnhardt was cast-iron and beat Waltrip for the championship by 288 points. *Dick Conway*

Earnhardt buzzes by the grandstand at Dover in September. A flat tire put him in the wall and left him 21st. Although it was one of only three finishes out of the top-20 all year, he maintained a 138-point lead over Tim Richmond in the season standings. *Dick Conway*

Earnhardt's pit crew (that's David Smith with the jack and Kirk Shelmerdine on the right-front) goes to work during the annual Unocal Pit Crew Competition at Rockingham. The Flying Aces won the 1986 event—their second of four in a row—with a stop in 27.601 seconds. *Bryant McMurray*

Earnhardt and Richard Childress share the big trophy after Earnhardt's dominating victory at Atlanta, that clinched the Winston Cup championship. The title was the first of six that the two men would share, and the first for Childress. *Bryant McMurray*

Earnhardt joins what amounts to an all-star game through the fourth turn at the 1987 Daytona 500, with Buddy Baker (88), Darrell Waltrip (17), and Richard Petty (43) also contending. Earnhardt led just one lap (during fuel stops). A slow fuel stop with 10 laps to go (in a mileage race) left him fifth at the finish. *Dick Conway*

In an all-time classic on the backstretch at Daytona, Earnhardt contends with Buddy Baker (88) and Darrell Waltrip (17). Baker was close to the end of his 30-year driving career, but his results were near the top of the all-time speed sheets. Earnhardt and Waltrip were fierce rivals for 15 years.
Dick Conway

Earnhardt took the points lead at Rockingham in February 1987 and never let up. He racked up a season for the ages. He won 11 races, had 21 top-fives, and clinched the trophy at Rockingham later that season with three races to go. No doubt, it was Earnhardt's most dominating season.
Dick Conway

THE KIRK SHELMERDINE ERA 1987

The No. 3 team, with crew chief Kirk Shelmerdine at center, begins reconstruction of the car Earnhardt crashed in practice at Richmond. With the car rebuilt, Earnhardt led 246 of the 500 laps and nailed his first victory in an outstanding season. *Dick Conway*

Earnhardt and Geoff Bodine (right) were never exactly friends, but everyone in NASCAR had to acknowledge the emergence of Bodine and car owner Rick Hendrick (center). Hendrick went on to equal Junior Johnson and Richard Childress as a record-breaking car owner, and won four championships with Jeff Gordon and one with Terry Labonte.
Dick Conway

Left: The Earnhardt icon—the hawk-like profile, narrowed eyes, and cocky smile—was fully developed by 1987. The persona went back to his father, Ralph, and his life in Kannapolis, North Carolina, which since has named streets after him. *Dick Conway*

Above: Three Champions. Earnhardt had a moment with Darrell Waltrip (center) and Rusty Wallace (right). Waltrip was the king in those days, with three championships to Earnhardt's two (three in 1987). Wallace was on the rise as champ in 1988. *Dick Conway*

Wrangler was the primary sponsor of the Richard Childress cars in 1987, but given the competitive climate in Detroit in the 1980s, General Motors decided it needed to field a factory team. The giant company settled on Childress and Earnhardt, and GM's Goodwrench division became the big sponsor in 1988. *Dick Conway*

The fall race at Richmond in 1987 ranks with the best in NASCAR history. For the last 80 laps, top rivals Earnhardt and Darrell Waltrip battled side-by-side, inside and outside. A caution near the end left Earnhardt the winner and the fans breathless. Waltrip shows the strain of the contest. *Dick Conway*

Weary from the all-out battle, Earnhardt nevertheless showed the satisfaction of winning after a hard fight. Dale's lead, with seven races to go, was a phenomenal 609 points, allowed him to claim the title without another win. *Dick Conway*

The first glance of the new black Goodwrench cars was at the pre-Daytona tests in 1988. Two of the black monsters, the cars that brought the Intimidator legend to full maturity, await tuning in the speedway's garages. *Dick Conway*

Earnhardt paces Sterling Marlin (44), Terry Labonte (11), Davey Allison (28), and Lake Speed (83), with Buddy Baker and Cale Yarborough trailing. This was the first "restricted" race at Daytona, and the unintended consequence of the 1-inch plate was that bunched cars into helpless packs. It was a whole new way of racing. *Dick Conway*

For once, Earnhardt was not the center of attention at Daytona when he finished 10th. The Tim Richmond controversy, the restrictor plates, the Tire War, Richard Petty's crash, and the one-two finish by father and son Bobby and Davey Allison took the headlines. Earnhardt calmly faced the press after a middling finish. *Dick Conway*

Neil Bonnett, driving the Rahmoc No. 75, laps Earnhardt at Richmond in February. Bonnett, who was still recovering from a badly fractured thigh suffered the year before at Charlotte, won at the old Fairgrounds track. Earnhardt finished 10th, a lap down. Bonnett was Earnhardt's closest friend, and his death at Daytona in 1994 shook the champ. *Dick Conway*

The Sunday line-up on a pleasant morning at Richmond. Earnhardt leads the second row ahead of Rusty Wallace and Harry Gant. Morgan Shepherd, on Hoosier tires, won the pole and started inside. The faster, stickier Hoosiers proved to be superior, especially on flat tracks. *Dick Conway*

Earnhardt battles Bobby Allison (12) at Richmond. Allison, one of the sport's true legends, went from the sport's highest peak (leading son Davey across the finish line at Daytona) to its lowest valley (his career-ending injuries at Pocono) in just four months. *Dick Conway*

Earnhardt scans the scene at Rockingham, the third race of the season. Neil Bonnett—who had chosen Hoosier tires, the rival to established Goodyear—won at Richmond, and again at Rockingham. The wins opened the eyes of Goodyear loyalists such as Earnhardt, who realized they had a war on their hands. *Dick Conway*

The name over the door says, "Dale Earnhardt," but the name on the helmet and the face behind it say, "David Pearson." Pearson, who hadn't yet officially retired, took a few laps in Dale's car at Richmond in September to test his aching back for a possible comeback. *Dick Conway*

Earnhardt, running both the Winston Cup and Busch races at Richmond, finds a quiet moment in his Busch hauler. Wife Teresa is in the background. Earnhardt always could nap on a moment's notice, and most who know racing understand that a night's sleep comes in installments. *Dick Conway*

Rising star Rusty Wallace (27) was the new kid on the block in 1988, when he became a points contender for the first time. The all-out, slap-dash approach of Wallace and the Raymond Beadle team was refreshing at the time. Wallace edged Earnhardt for the championship in 1989. *Dick Conway*

Geoff Bodine, from Elmira, New York, was one of the first Yankee invaders to make some noise in the big leagues. For whatever reasons, he and Earnhardt were fierce adversaries through the 1980s, notably at The Winston in 1987. Bodine also took the Daytona 500 win from Earnhardt in 1986, which Dale later said was his most bitter disappointment. *Dick Conway*

Darrell Waltrip (17) had to wait nearly as long as Earnhardt for his first Daytona 500 victory. Waltrip, three-time champion, won on his 17th try. It took seven-time champion Earnhardt 20 tries to win his first Daytona 500. *Dick Conway*

In early 1989, the first Goodyear-Hoosier "tire war" was at its peak, and some teams adjusted better than others did. Although fiercely loyal to Goodyear, Earnhardt and many others were forced to qualify on Hoosiers at Richmond. They switched back to Goodyears when the Hoosiers began to blister in practice. *Dick Conway*

Although Earnhardt downplayed his kinder nature, he always was willing to pitch in to help anyone who needed it. At Daytona in 1989, Earnhardt offered advice and a hand to budding Busch Series racer Elton Sawyer. *Dick Conway*

THE KIRK SHELMERDINE ERA 1989

As his career progressed, Earnhardt became increasingly comfortable with the big brokers and heavyweights. The man on the left is multi-time Indy 500 winner Roger Penske, an emperor in industry and in racing. *Dick Conway*

General Motors debuted its red-black-silver color scheme for its Goodwrench division in 1987. RCR, GM's flagship team, personified the colors. For several years, the cockpits of the No. 3 cars were painted red, as opposed to the standard primer gray. *Dick Conway*

THE KIRK SHELMERDINE ERA 1989

Earnhardt's Flying Aces crew, led by chief Kirk Shelmerdine (front tires), David Smith (jack), Chocolate Myers (fuel), and Will Lind, revolutionized pit work in the late 1980s. Through careful analysis and practice, the Aces lowered their pit stop time by five seconds in two years and won the Unocal contest at Rockingham four years in a row. *Dick Conway*

THE KIRK SHELMERDINE ERA 1989

The Chevrolet teams began the season with the old fastback Monte Carlos, but in an unusual midseason model change, they switched to the new Lumina at Talladega in the spring. The Lumina was used for five years and was never as good as the older car. RCR nevertheless whipped the Lumina into shape and won three times with that car, and once in the Monte Carlo. *Dick Conway*

No one should underestimate the influence of Teresa Earnhardt in Dale's life and career. The niece of veteran Busch Series racer Tommy Houston, Teresa married Dale in November 1982. She was Dale's soul mate, and he always deferred to her intelligence, business sense, and attention to detail. *Dick Conway*

Earnhardt jumped out of the Richmond pits ahead of Bill Elliott (9), Ken Schrader (25), Rusty Wallace (27), and Geoff Bodine (5). In the early fall of 1989, Earnhardt won Darlington, was second at Richmond, and won Dover all in a row. A broken camshaft at Charlotte in October, however, yielded the points lead to eventual champion Wallace. *Dick Conway*

By 1989, long shot Alan Kulwicki, who in 1985 came south from Wisconsin with a race car and a tow trailer, had become a player to be reckoned with—especially when it came to qualifying. Kulwicki went on to win an inspiring championship in 1992. A tragic plane crash took his life in early 1993. *Dick Conway*

THE KIRK SHELMERDINE ERA 1989

Earnhardt blazes out of the pits during green-flag stops near halfway. Dale led 144 of the 200 laps, and endured one of the most famous and improbable calamities of his Daytona career: a flat tire in the last turn of the last lap. The trophy went to Derrike Cope, who had Buddy Parrott in the pits. *Dick Conway*

Earnhardt's work in the Busch Series was almost forgotten in his record at Daytona. He won seven Goody's 300s at the big track, including five in a row from 1990 to 1994. In 1990, he readied for the start outside pole-winner Darrell Waltrip (17). *Dick Conway*

As with many under constant scrutiny, Earnhardt had ways of creating solitude for himself and finding time to think. Even while he carried on conversations, Earnhardt could multitask, talking about one thing while reflecting on something else. *Dick Conway*

THE KIRK SHELMERDINE ERA 1990

Earnhardt, who had not won a championship since 1987, began the 1990 season on a mission. In reference to the 1988 and 1989 seasons, he declared, "They kind of caught the cat sleeping a little bit." After a tough month of June, Earnhardt hit his stride and won three of four, beginning at Michigan. He finished out of the top-10 only once the rest of the year. *Dick Conway*

Hot-shot Davey Allison (28) was still a year away from contention, even though he won rookie-of-the-year honors in 1987. Allison was a tough competitor and would have been a worthy rival to Earnhardt and Jeff Gordon in the 1990s. *Dick Conway*

NO PRISONERS

By Jonathan Ingram

Dale Earnhardt loved to watch Formula 1 racing on the TV in his motorhome on Sundays prior to Winston Cup events. He said this the night he received the Gregor Grant Award for lifetime achievement from *Autosport* at the magazine's awards banquet in London in 1996, amid the luminaries in Grand Prix racing. "Watching the F1 races helps me get prepared for what I have to do later in the day," he said.

The *Autosport* Awards took place in the huge Grosvenor House ballroom, a room big enough to dwarf the Waldorf Astoria, where the Winston Cup hosts its post-season banquet. Nearly all the participants in the major motor racing series sanctioned by the Federation Internationale de l'Automobile (FIA), racing's international governing body, attend the *Autosport* Awards. It was still a surprise when former F1 driver Martin Brundle joined Earnhardt on the podium to talk about the one very brief meeting he'd had with the stock car racing champion.

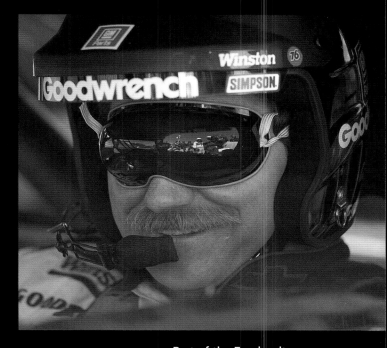

Brundle was contesting the International Race of Champions (IROC) championship in 1990 versus Earnhardt, and had won a round on the airport circuit in Cleveland, the second foreign-born driver to appear in victory lane at the all-star series. Earnhardt finished fifth in Cleveland after starting last due to his victory at Talladega. "I was just trying to be smooth," said Earnhardt, "and then get 'em at Michigan."

The Englishman was all smiles as he told his story about starting the last race of the series at the Michigan International Speedway oval with the points lead. Brundle's wife was close to delivering a child at the time. "I'll never forget the first five words Dale Earnhardt said to me," recalled Brundle. "He walked past my car on the starting grid and said, 'Remember the wife and kid.'

The road racer spun and crashed early in that Michigan race. Earnhardt won the race and the second of his four IROC championships.

Part of the Earnhardt appeal was his retro driving gear. By 1990, most drivers had gone to full-face helmets. Earnhardt persisted in wearing the tank helmet with goggles. Some believed the open-face ensemble was what allowed him to "see the air," or at least to feel it, at the drafting tracks.
Dick Conway

THE KIRK SHELMERDINE ERA 1990

Earnhardt dismisses Ernie Irvan (4) on the way to second place at Richmond in September. As in the case of young Allison, observers can wonder what the following decade would have been like had Irvan not been hurt. *Dick Conway*

The 1990 points battle was one of NASCAR's most memorable. Earnhardt and the emerging Mark Martin were never more than 50 points apart down the stretch. Martin and crew panicked in the finale at Atlanta and borrowed a car from Robert Yates and finished sixth. Earnhardt, with his eyes on the prize, finished fifth and won his fourth Cup. *Dick Conway*

What Earnhardt had promised at the start of the 1990 season came true at its end. After two shut-out years, Earnhardt returned to the top of the sport with his fourth Winston Cup. Daughter Taylor (right), not yet two, learned that what glitters can truly be golden. *Bryant McMurray*

Earnhardt leads Darrell Waltrip (17), Ernie Irvan (4), and Sterling Marlin (22) through the tri-oval in the 1991 Daytona 500. Earnhardt and Davey Allison battled for second behind Irvan, Dale but spun out with three to go, and left Irvan with his first and biggest NASCAR victory. *Dick Conway*

Earnhardt, firmly in the lead with 10 laps to go in the 1991 Daytona 500, tangled with challenger Davey Allison while the pair ran for second with three laps to go. Earnhardt's chances for victory had vanished as he coasted, scarred and smoking, to the pits. *Bryant McMurray*

Team owner Richard Childress is master of all he surveys from the top of the Goodwrench hauler at Daytona. Although Childress and Earnhardt often butted heads, they had a kinship, and yielded to each other's brilliance. *Dick Conway*

Earnhardt paces Bill Elliott, Darrell Waltrip, Morgan Shepherd, and Michael Waltrip at Talladega in May. Earnhardt couldn't match Harry Gant's fuel mileage and finished third, but he took the points lead from Ricky Rudd. *Bryant McMurray*

Earnhardt goes side-by-side with Sterling Marlin off the fourth turn at Charlotte in October. He fell out with a broken valve after 302 laps and finished 25th. In a points race no one seemed to want to win, Earnhardt expanded his lead over Ricky Rudd to 138. *Nigel Kinrade*

Earnhardt hoists the Winston Cup at Atlanta, where he only had to start to clinch his fifth championship. Wife Teresa and daughter Taylor are to Dale's right, and R. J. Reynolds impresario T. Wayne Robertson is to his left. Suddenly, Richard Petty's record of seven Cups seemed to be in sight. *Nigel Kinrade*

Kirk Shelmerdine, son of a Philadelphia computer salesman, guided four of Earnhardt's championships. Tired of the pace, Shelmerdine "retired" after 1992. When he had the money and the urge, Shelmerdine went on to race his own cars in sportsman, ARCA, and even Winston Cup. *Bryant McMurray*

Richard Petty (43), who began racing in 1959, was NASCAR's hero for a generation. By 1991, Earnhardt had become the new icon. Even the most dedicated Petty supporters urged the 54-year-old King to stand down, which he did after the 1992 season. *Bryant McMurray*

The 1992 Daytona 500 introduced the term "The Big One" to describe one hazard of restricted racing. A tangle among Ernie Irvan, Sterling Marlin, and Bill Elliott caused a 14-car wreck. Davey Allison led 95 of the last 100 laps to win, and Earnhardt, who sustained some damage in the wreck, finished ninth. *Nigel Kinrade*

Earnhardt's all-star crew, including chief Kirk Shelmerdine (front right) and veteran Chocolate Myers (with the gas can), service the No. 3 car at Darlington, where Earnhardt finished 10th. GM Goodwrench's dark identity in the early 1990s helped cement Earnhardt's "Intimidator" reputation. *Nigel Kinrade*

Earnhardt completes a green-flag stop at Darlington as future NBC commentator Wally Dallenbach (left) rolls into the pit lane. Earnhardt's car carried a roof camera, evidence of television's increasing presence in the sport by 1992. *Nigel Kinrade*

At Charlotte in May, Earnhardt pulled from his hat what turned out to be his only victory of 1992. This was not a dominating victory. Alan Kulwicki and Kyle Petty were the top contenders. Earnhardt, however, emerged at the end, and took the lead on Lap 347 of 400. Unocal's Bill Brodrick and TBS' Dick Berggren are to Earnhardt's left. *Nigel Kinrade*

Earnhardt and engine chief Ed Lanier survey the environment during some downtime as the 1992 season shifted into second gear. This was a strange season. Earnhardt and Davey Allison were the top contenders before Allison was badly hurt in a wreck at Pocono in July. Out of nowhere, miracle man Alan Kulwicki claimed the Cup at the end. *Nigel Kinrade*

THE
ANDY PETREE &
DAVID SMITH ERA

1993–1996

SEVENTH HEAVEN

By Jonathan Ingram

Dale Earnhardt rocked the house and the history books when he clinched his seventh Winston Cup in 1994 when he won the race at Rockingham, North Carolina. This crowning glory tied him with Richard Petty as the all-time leader in championships and gave the Childress team six titles in the preceding nine years.

It was much like the Boston Celtics or the New York Yankees celebrating yet another championship. "We stayed around the garage for a little while afterward and said, 'Ho-hum another championship,'" said crew chief Andy Petree, who added that not finishing second meant more to Earnhardt. "I don't think Dale liked winning nearly as much as he hated losing," said Petree. "He couldn't stand it when anybody beat him."

Earnhardt won the pole at Talladega in April 1993 and led the field to the green flag at the Alabama track's unique first-turn starting line. Earnhardt finished fourth in the Winston 500, and then went on a tear, and won five of the next nine races to seize the points lead.
Nigel Kinrade

A different sort of loss earlier that year turned an otherwise sunny, hot day in the North Carolina Sandhills with the hint of tragedy. The celebration was muted because the race win was dedicated to Neil Bonnett, Earnhardt's fishing buddy and only close friend among drivers. Earlier in 1994, Bonnett had been killed in an accident aboard a Chevy owned by James Finch. The accident caused by suspension failure, occurred during practice for the Daytona 500. Earnhardt and Childress had encouraged Bonnett's return to the Winston Cup the year before, and let him drive Dale's back-up cars at Talladega and Atlanta. These were Bonnett's first entries in over three years after a serious head injury in 1990.

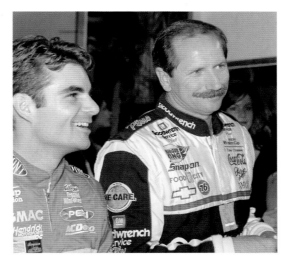

"Neil was such a good guy. That was a sad deal," said Petree. "And it was such a shock just before qualifying. We all got into the plane and went up to his funeral. Dale didn't dwell on things like that. By time we got to the Daytona 500 he was ready to race."

Earnhardt and the Childress crew showed up ready to win the season championship. "One of the things I liked about Dale, and I think made him a great race car driver, was that he was always fresh when he came to the race track," said Petree. "He didn't spend his time thinking about shocks or springs or Ford-versus-Chevy. When he left the race track he was on his farm, he was hunting, he'd spend time with his family, but he was not thinking about racin'. I think that's why he never burnt out. I always wondered how somebody could be The Man for so many years? That's how he did it."

Earnhardt didn't care much for pre-race car set-up, or even qualifying, said Petree. "I don't know how many times he told me, 'You just load the wagon. I'll drive it.'"

Not even the mounting wins of Rusty Wallace for Roger Penske or the hot start by Ernie Irvan in his first full season as the replacement for Davey Allison in the Robert Yates Ford could dampen the Childress team's confidence. "When I was there, Richard Childress Racing and Dale were the team to beat," said Petree. "We really didn't look at anybody else. We never once focused on any other team. The only thing we focused on was us."

Irvan held first both in miles led and bonus points for leading the most laps when a horrendous, near-fatal practice crash at Michigan in August took him out of the championship derby. "A lot of people thought Ernie was ahead in the points at the time of his accident," said Petree. "But we were leading. Ernie would have had his work cut out for him in my opinion."

Long after dark, in the fall race at Atlanta, Earnhardt celebrated his sixth championship. He finished tenth in what then was called the Hooters 500. This was good enough to hold off race-winner Rusty Wallace by 80 points in the final tally. *Nigel Kinrade*

There was a letdown following Irvan's departure, acknowledged Petree. It was also apparent to the crew. "There was a big problem with Ernie," said Brad Francis, a team member who worked on technical development. "Ernie was strong, real strong, and the Yates team was fast. Yates had a lot of horsepower and the car was flying at Michigan. That accident affected Earnhardt, I think. Being in the points race with Rusty was not as difficult. He'd mess around with Rusty all day long. Ernie was different because Yates had faster equipment. It made the championship hollow."

By time the Childress team rolled into Rockingham, critics in the media and elsewhere pointed out Earnhardt's lack of victories. They also accused him of chasing points. The idea was to win , but not sacrifice a championship, said Petree. "Nobody in the sport that I ever saw was better at scoring points than Dale," he said. "Rusty Wallace could win more races, but Dale won the championships. If he had to lead laps, he'd try hard to do it, but he wouldn't take chances on leading laps and wreck the car where he couldn't finish with it."

Wallace had won eight races compared to three by Earnhardt when they came into Rockingham. Early in the race, Earnhardt ignored the pressure from the media concerning a lack of victories. He even cut a deal with friend Ken Schrader, who let him take the lead for a lap early in the event to get the five bonus points. Earnhardt promptly gave it back, letting those in the press box know that he didn't give a damn about their opinion of his strategy of consistent finishes and points gathering.

Then, when Wallace fell out with engine trouble and the championship was all but clinched, Earnhardt went to work, ready to win the title his way. Maybe the wagon—his black GM Goodwrench Chevy—wasn't quite loaded as well as usual, which meant he had

THE RADIAL EFFECT

By Jonathan Ingram

While Earnhardt knew how to get the most out of bias ply tires, adapting to the new Goodyear radials is what won the titles for Earnhardt in 1993 and again in 1994. Earnhardt finds another use for the Goodyears in the Atlanta pits in November 1997. *Nigel Kinrade*

His pure control of the car was instrumental to Earnhardt's first five titles. He knew how to get the most out of bias ply tires, and whose optimum performance occurred when maximum pressure was applied by a tail-happy driving style. Adapting to the new Goodyear radials is what won the titles for Earnhardt in 1993 and again in 1994. It was a project directed by Petree, who had taken over for the departed Kirk Shelmerdine following a one-win campaign by Earnhardt in 1992.

"The bias ply tires operated at a lot higher slip angle," said Petree. "There was only a handful of guys who could hang 'em out that far to get the most out of them. Harry Gant, Cale Yarborough, and Dale Earnhardt are three that come to mind. You can't do that with radials. But great race car drivers will do whatever it takes to figure it out. Dale didn't care what it took, he just wanted to beat that other guy."

Earnhardt adjusted to radials slowly during the 1993 season, which started with a loss to Dale Jarrett on the last lap of the Daytona 500 because Jarrett did a better job of saving his tires with more gradual corner entries and faster exits. At New Hampshire that year, this gentler technique became clear to Earnhardt when he lost his brakes on the one-mile flat oval.

"We completely lost the brakes," said Petree. "But we were turning competitive lap times. He was killin' people comin' off the corners. I'd tell him (over the radio), 'Dale, pay attention to what's goin' on. Watch this.' If he'd of had brakes, he'd a been drivin' it in there and then gotten beat off the corners."

Dale, wife Teresa, and daughter Taylor celebrate as Earnhardt lugs the 1993 Winston Cup out of victory lane at Atlanta. Suddenly, Richard Petty's all-time record of seven championships was in sight, and Earnhardt and his crew had already begun to power up for a charge in 1994. *Nigel Kinrade*

a bigger job carrying it. It was an unseasonably hot day for Rockingham that made the track slick, which wore out all the chauffeurs. Perhaps knowing that the title would be dedicated to Bonnett, there might have been more emotion pulling at Earnhardt, especially given the history-making element of a seventh Winston Cup. For whatever reason, Earnhardt was not fresh as the 492-lap race wore on at the high-banked, D-shaped mile oval.

Earnhardt would lead the final 76 laps, but not without encouragement from the pits. The man to beat was Rick Mast, who had been busy recovering from a mid-race accident. "It was such a hot day and Dale was falling out of the seat," said Petree. "He was trying to hold his head up. It was the most I ever talked to him on the radio during a race. I kept tellin' him Rick was coming, that he would be hard to beat and I kept givin' him the lap times."

The enormous effort showed when Earnhardt bobbled in Turn 3 on the final lap before beating Mast by half a car length. "I was trying to get as close to him as I could," said Mast afterward, "and then tuck under him to take the air off his spoiler." It didn't work, because the wily Earnhardt moved up the track. "Dale stayed up on that wheel and beat him," said Petree. "That was not an easy win."

While Petree drove the Childress Chevy into victory lane, aboard the victory trailer used by Winston for the championship celebration, Earnhardt acknowledged Bonnett and then Petty, whom he declared "will always be The King."

Inevitably, the question arose later in the press box. Had his feelings about Bonnett's death interfered with his season? Nobody present could remember the voice of the "The Intimidator" ever cracking with emotion before. "It interfered more with my fishin'," Earnhardt replied quietly. "I can't go fishin' on my own lake any more because of Neil."

THE ANDY PETREE & DAVID SMITH ERA 1993

PUSHING THE ENVELOPE

By Jonathan Ingram

To think of Dale Earnhardt, "The Intimidator," as a sensitive guy, well that almost seems absurd. Although according to Brad Francis, a technical guru with Richard Childress Racing, Earnhardt had incredible sensitivity to a car's handling.

"During the Coca-Cola 600 in 1993," said Francis, "Dale came on the radio and said, 'I wish the track bar was down a quarter of an inch.' He could read the car's performance in a heartbeat."

Francis knew that the bar located under the chassis at the rear of the car was instrumental to Earnhardt's car set-ups, because it dramatically affected the roll center, or weight movement, in the corners. "I decided to go to work on it," said Francis. "How can we put the track bar up or down quickly during a pit stop? It made such an impression that Dale was pissed off about this."

By Monday at noon, Francis had built a device to raise or lower the track bar in increments of 1/16th of an inch. He showed it to Earnhardt. "Get it on my car! That's what I want!" said the driver enthusiastically. By the following weekend, the Childress entry carried the unit, which was adjusted by a long ratchet wrench inserted through a hole in the rear window. Other teams would have to get under the car on pit stops, undo, and then re-do a set of bolts to make changes of 1/8th of an inch or more. It was not only a less-accurate process, but also far more time consuming than Francis' invention.

"We were the only ones who had it for about 90 days," said Francis. "We hid it as much as we possibly could. Then Steve Hmiel of Roush Racing, who was always good in scoping out other cars, saw it." From there, the adjustable track bar became a standard piece of equipment on all cars in the Winston Cup. Typically, Earnhardt had pushed the envelope for everybody.

The color and clamor of pit stops under caution provide a feverish show unequaled in sports. The crew goes to work on Earnhardt's Chevrolet at Martinsville, where he started eighth and finished 11th, a lap down. By the 1994 season, the adjustable track bar pioneered by Earnhardt the previous season was standard equipment. *Nigel Kinrade*

Earnhardt and Ernie
Irvan (28) chase Todd
Bodine's lapped car
through the fourth turn
in the 1994 Daytona
500. Irvan, who had left
Morgan-McClure to join
Robert Yates, quickly
became Earnhardt's top
rival in the 1994 title
chase. Ironically, Sterling
Marlin, who replaced
Irvan in No. 4, won the
500, with Irvan in
second. *Nigel Kinrade*

Eyes straight ahead,
Earnhardt waits
out a pit stop at
Darlington in late March.
The spring race at the
ancient speedway was
reduced to 400
miles in 1994, and
Earnhardt paced
properly to capture his
first trophy of 1994.
Nigel Kinrade

With his voice gaining a grievous edge, Earnhardt continued. "We fished in it all the time.
I try. Ain't no fun."

Once again, it had been a season where Earnhardt and the Childress team had stead-fastly refused to beat themselves under any circumstances. The year started with the fatal accident of his close friend and then appeared to end prematurely when Irvan nearly died at Michigan. In the latter half of the season, the Wallace's wins began mounting, as did criticism from the media about Earnhardt's uncharacteristic lack of aggression. Losing a friend to a fatal accident was something Earnhardt couldn't control, nor could he control the near-fatal accident of his chief competitor. But beating himself in a championship chase? That would never happen.

THE ANDY PETREE & DAVID SMITH ERA 1994

After a slow start, Earnhardt knocked off back-to-back victories at Darlington (shown here) and Bristol. Another victory at Talladega three tries later propelled Earnhardt into a dogfight with Ernie Irvan for the points lead. *Nigel Kinrade*

Earnhardt leads Mark Martin, Kle Petty, and Earnie Irvan into the first turn at the tight and tough Martinsville Speedway, a true street-fighters track. This was early in the race, and cars do not have a scratch on them. They won't stay that way for long. *Nigel Kinrade*

THE ANDY PETREE & DAVID SMITH ERA 1994

Right: Earnhardt sails down the front straight during the inaugural Brickyard 400, NASCAR's breakthrough race at Indianapolis Motor Speedway. Earnhardt was a contender all day and finished fifth. Jeff Gordon took the top laurels in one of the most significant events in NASCAR history. *Nigel Kinrade*

Below: Earnhardt leads Ernie Irvan into the uphill chicane at the Watkins Glen course. The next week at Michigan, Irvan, the top contender in points, was gravely injured in a wreck that left Earnhardt without a challenger for the season's title. *Nigel Kinrade*

THE ANDY PETREE & DAVID SMITH ERA 1994

BOY WONDER

By Jonathan Ingram

The Winston Cup champion who grew up in the North Carolina mill town of Kannapolis eventually had a lot of respect for Jeff Gordon, but that didn't stop him from giving the kid from Indiana his derisive nickname in 1994. A multimillion-dollar bonus baby for Rick Hendrick, Gordon had crashed 10 times in his rookie season in 1993. Early the next season, he showed signs of improvement when he qualified third at Rockingham.

"Richard was up on the truck clocking the other cars in the first practice," said Petree. "I said, 'How 'bout boy wonder, what's he running?' I said it just like that on the radio. There was this whole buzz about Jeff Gordon back then. Everybody, including Earnhardt, who was in the car, started laughing when I said it. Gordon didn't qualify on the pole, but Dale made this statement about 'Wonder Boy.' He was trying to repeat this statement I had made and got it wrong. So that's how he ended up getting the name. Dale started talking about Wonder Boy to the media."

Earnhardt clinched his record-tying seventh Winston Cup championship by winning at Rockingham in October 1994 with three weeks left in the season. The victory ended a streak of seven top-three finishes in eight races. The final margin was 444 points, the fourth-largest in Cup history to that time. *Nigel Kinrade*

Earnhardt and crew chief Andy Petree remained perfect through 1994 —two years, two championships. Both men were strong-willed, and their aims did not always coincide, but where the ultimate goal was concerned —winning races and championships—the pairing was exactly right. *Nigel Kinrade*

Earnhardt made history in 1994 when he tied Richard Petty's record of seven championships, once thought to be unapproachable. Yet, Earnhardt felt that the victory was hollow because the injuries to Ernie Irvan left him without a real challenger. Through the last third of the season, Earnhardt was virtually alone at the top. *Nigel Kinrade*

Earnhardt drove the car, but owner Richard Childress, as always, steered the ship. The 1994 season gave Childress his sixth championship, all with Earnhardt. Through a fabulous, 11-year run, the title years came in pairs: 1986–1987, 1990–1991, and 1993–1994.
Nigel Kinrade

Earnhardt gets the jump on the field at the start of the 1995 Daytona 500, towing Sterling Marlin (4) toward the front as pole-winner Dale Jarrett, in the Texaco car, settles into line. Marlin led the most laps of the race and took the lead from Earnhardt with 20 laps to go. *Nigel Kinrade*

Earnhardt and Dale Jarrett were at the peak of their superspeedway rivalry in 1995. The Chevrolet-Ford competition was also at a fevered pitch, as Chevy introduced its new Monte Carlo. Jarrett and Earnhardt, who qualified one-two at Daytona, scream past the grandstand into Turn 1. *Nigel Kinrade*

Right: Earnhardt continued to add feathers to his Daytona cap when he won the opening IROC round for the fourth time in six years. This one ended in controversy when Earnhardt crashed Al Unser Jr. out of the lead on the last lap. The wreck was not intentional, and Earnhardt was shaken by the turn of events. *Nigel Kinrade*

Above: Smoke boils from hot tires and cooked brakes as the crew goes to work. Earnhardt's spot-on pit crew got him to the lead with 37 laps to go in the 1995 Daytona 500, but Sterling Marlin had too much muscle and ran down Dale with 20 laps to go. It was Earnhardt's second second-place finish in three years. *Nigel Kinrade*

SAVE ME SOME FUEL

By Jonathan Ingram

Dale Earnhardt invariably ran a race the way he wanted to, guided by only his own conscience and the seat of his pants. "Ninety-nine percent of the time, he was doing what he wanted to do," said crew chief Andy Petree. "That's the way he ran the race. We didn't talk much on the radio."

One of the few exceptions came in the 1995 season finale in Atlanta, where Jeff Gordon clinched his first title—and snubbed Earnhardt's effort to win a record-tying three straight championship and a record eighth overall. With a little less than 75 miles to go, Earnhardt led the race by 18 seconds. "He was trying to make a statement since Jeff had beaten him to the championship," said Petree.

In the pits, the Childress team was worried about gas mileage. "Our numbers told us we couldn't make it," said Petree, who had already talked with his driver at various times during their three years together about how to save fuel. "Dale had asked and I had told him some of the things that Harry Gant would do," said Petree, who had come to Childress from the Leo Jackson team. "But they weren't consistent with Dale's driving style. To save gas, you had to back off early (from the throttle), use very little brake, and give it the least throttle as you can to make the lap time.

"In Atlanta, I told him we were going to be close on our fuel mileage and that we were going to have to stretch our mileage on our next two runs. One run, then a pit stop, and then one more run to the finish. I told him we had to make up two or three laps, or we can't make it [to the finish under green].

"You could see him driving into the corners real hard from the pit wall in Atlanta. So I told him, 'Dale you need to save some fuel.' He said, 'Yeah, yeah.' Then he ran out of fuel one lap before I wanted him to come in and he coasts into the pits and then goes back out.

"I'm on the radio again. 'Okay, Dale. Gotta save me some fuel.' He started getting a little short. 'Dammit I'm saving fuel.'

"Finally, I said, 'You've got an 18-second lead and saving a little bit of fuel won't hurt.' 'Dammit!' he said 'I've been saving fuel.'

"Usually I would just let him blow some steam and I wouldn't say anything back, but I had to this time because we weren't going to make it. I said, 'We need to slow down about two-tenths of a lap.' And he still wouldn't slow down. I said, 'Dale, slow down.' Again, he'd start cussin'.

"I said, 'Dale, it doesn't matter how much you win by. They still pay you the same.' He finally slowed down and we won that race and we didn't have two tea cups full of gas left in it."

That was a typical experience working with Earnhardt, said Petree, who found that one of his driver's weaknesses was trying to do too many things at one time. Sometimes he'd ignore his race car during the weekend and instead spend most of his time cutting business deals. In the case of the Atlanta race, he was trying to send a message about the championship in addition to trying to win. "He would listen to you if you really pushed him," said Petree. "He might cuss a little bit. Sometimes he'd bark right back at you and you'd feel like crap. Then he'd do what you were talkin' about.

"But he really would've looked bad if he had run out of gas while leading that race in Atlanta."

As it was, Earnhardt led 268 of 328 laps and finished with an average speed of 163.633 miles per hour, which remained the track record for six years. He won by 3.74 seconds over Sterling Marlin after his chief com-

The field pits under caution at Rockingham. Never a great qualifier, Earnhardt started 23rd at The Rock, but he had the No. 1 pit box through the entire season as the defending champion. That and the superb RCR pit crew made up for a dozen qualifying positions every time out. *Nigel Kinrade*

At Rockingham in 1995, Earnhardt took the points lead with a third-place finish and held it through April. New challenger Jeff Gordon, however, stepped into the spotlight and dominated the Goodwrench 500. Here, Dale dismisses the lapped cars of Dick Trickle (15) and Jeff Burton (8), with Mark Martin and Bill Elliott behind him. *Nigel Kinrade*

The three-year association of Earnhardt and crew chief Andy Petree was fruitful. Together they won back-to-back championships, 15 races, and 9 poles. At the time of the Talladega race in April, Petree had already was considering becoming a team owner, and in 1995 he took over Leo Jackson's operation. *Nigel Kinrade*

At Darlington in late March, Earnhardt finished second. He began the year with five top-fours in a row. Seen here in the garage during practice, Earnhardt has the look of a man who expects to win every time out. *Nigel Kinrade*

Earnhardt was either unbeatable or cursed throughout 1995. The curses began to accumulate in April with setbacks in the races at Bristol and Martinsville (shown here). Over Earnhardt's right shoulder is Jeff Gordon, who had won three times by April, and finished third at the Martinsville half-mile. *Nigel Kinrade*

Earnhardt helps the crew push the car out of the garage before time trials at Talladega in April. The team's mid-spring slump continued when Earnhardt qualified 16th and finished 21st, which was his third April result out of the top-20. *Nigel Kinrade*

For a roughneck kid from Kannapolis, North Carolina, victory at the fabled Speedway was an amazing achievement. Earnhardt accepts congratulations from Speedway president Tony George (right) as the victory celebration begins. *Nigel Kinrade*

Earnhardt won on the return trip to Martinsville in September and beat Terry Labonte and April winner Rusty Wallace (seen here). Earnhardt finished with a streak of 8 top-fives in 10 races to keep the heat on points leader Jeff Gordon. *Nigel Kinrade*

The Atlanta finale was a triumphant show of defiance by Earnhardt, crew chief Andy Petree (left), and car owner Richard Childress (right). Although Jeff Gordon wilted down the stretch, he clinched the season title at Atlanta. Earnhardt dominated the race and led 268 of the 328 laps to finish the year with an exclamation point. *Nigel Kinrade*

Old adversaries Bill Elliott and Earnhardt have a friendly discussion during 1996 Speed Weeks preparations. To Earnhardt's right is Elliott's wife, Cindy. To Elliott's left is Mike Beam, crew chief of Elliott's No. 94. Earnhardt is leaning on Dale Jarrett's car. *Nigel Kinrade*

Earnhardt and crew had probably never been more prepared for Daytona than in 1996. Earnhardt stormed to the Beach and won the pole. In the end, Ford's Dale Jarrett used superior muscle to hold off Earnhardt at the end. Referring to an engine variance given to Ford over the winter, Earnhardt complained, "They gave 'em the candy store." *Nigel Kinrade*

Earnhardt certainly had reason to be pleased. His 1996 Speed Weeks was one of his best. He kicked it off by winning his first-ever Daytona 500 pole, won his qualifying heat (of course), and added a win in Thursday's IROC race. The final kick, however, was another bitterly disappointing second place in the big race, his third in four years. *Nigel Kinrade*

THE ANDY PETREE & DAVID SMITH ERA 1996

On a typical chilly afternoon at Bristol in late March, Earnhardt and crew commenced an amazing streak of seven top-fives in a row, which vaulted him to the lead in points. Owner Richard Childress, in characteristic boss pose, eyes the action from the top of the pit box. Earnhardt finished fourth on the high banks. *Nigel Kinrade*

David Smith, who had been with owner Richard Childress through thick and thin since 1980, shared crew chief duties with longtime teammate Bobby Hutchens in 1995 and 1996. This unique relationship continued until Larry McReynolds was hired at the end of the season. *Nigel Kinrade*

Earnhardt waits out corner-weight and a tire change in his office during practice at North Wilkesboro in April. Earnhardt won five times at North Wilkesboro before the .625-mile antique was closed for good after the fall race. In the spring event, he started 26th and finished 3rd. *Nigel Kinrade*

Earnhardt shares a laugh with NASCAR VP of Competition Mike Helton (center) and ascendant superstar Jeff Gordon in the Talladega garage in July. This race ended with Earnhardt's terrifying and crippling crash on the front stretch, which probably cost him the championship. *Nigel Kinrade*

No race exemplified Earnhardt's determination more than the Watkins Glen event in August, which was two weeks after the Talladega crash. Earnhardt ached with a broken sternum and collarbone, but won the pole in record time and led a race-high 54 laps. It would prove to be the last pole he ever won. *Nigel Kinrade*

Earnhardt leads Dale Jarrett and Ricky Rudd through the esses at Watkins Glen. Years later, fans still wore "Hurts So Good" T-shirts to commemorate Earnhardt's inspiring run that August afternoon. Nearly in tears when he was taken out of the car the previous week at Indy, Earnhardt wasn't about to let that happen again. *Nigel Kinrade*

The Charlotte race in October was a milepost on Earnhardt's late-season rally. He started 34th and finished 6th. It was his fourth top-10 in five races. But all that effort was too little, too late because Terry Labonte cemented his hold on the championship with the Charlotte trophy. *Nigel Kinrade*

Earnhardt later admitted that he tried too hard too soon after Talladega, but he was determined to tough it out at the time. With the pain all but gone, Earnhardt prepares to start the No. 3 in the Southern 500 at Darlington. *Nigel Kinrade*

Earnhardt steers through the north turns at Rockingham in October on the way to ninth place. The 1996 season was one of Earnhardt's most controversial. Observers debated whether the Talladega wreck cost him the championship and led to the long losing streak that followed. *Nigel Kinrade*

THE
LARRY McREYNOLDS ERA

1997–1998

THE DAYTONA FILES

By Al Pearce

At first, crew chief Larry McReynolds didn't know what to make of the unfamiliar voice in the headset of his two-way radio. There he was, trying to win NASCAR's most important race while someone who didn't belong on his channel kept cutting in and talking to his driver. Wired like a stick of dynamite with a short fuse, McReynolds was about to tell the voice identifying himself as "Captain Jack" to get off his channel and leave his team alone.

Instead, he caught a glimpse of team owner Richard Childress, standing nearby, frantically waving his arms and shaking his head. "It was like he was telling me, 'No, no. *Please* don't say anything on the radio,'" McReynolds said years later. "I was about to go ballistic and cuss out whoever was on my radio. Thankfully, Richard made me realize who it was. If I hadn't seen him waving, no telling what I would have said to the guy."

"Captain Jack," of course, was NASCAR president and chairman of the board Bill France Jr.

He was talking to Dale Earnhardt, addressing his longtime fishing buddy and good friend as "Sunday Money."

The race was the 1998 Daytona 500 at Daytona International Speedway. The date was February 15.

France, high above the track in Race Control, switched his two-way radio to the McReynolds-Childress-Earnhardt channel under the race's next-to-last caution. Only 25 laps remained, and Earnhardt was in a familiar position: Leading in the final laps of the Daytona 500, the only meaningful race he'd never won.

"So there we were, still leading after our last pit stop, getting ready for the restart," McReynolds said. "We'd just made a two-tire stop and had plenty of gas. I was pretty uptight right about then, when this voice came on the radio.

"It said something like, 'Hey, Sunday Money, this is Captain Jack.'

"Dale clicked back on and said, 'Go ahead, Captain Jack.' Man, I'm just about to explode because my driver is talking to somebody and I don't know who it is or what's going on.

"Then this other voice says, 'Looks like a good day to finally snag that big one.'

"Dale says back, 'We're gonna give it all we have, Captain Jack.' That's about when I'm ready to say something to this 'Captain Jack' fellow when I see Richard waving at me to keep quiet. Frankly, I didn't see the humor in any of it.

"But I should have known who it was. The year before, when I first went to work for Richard and Dale, the crew told me that Bill sometimes switched on our channel and talked to Dale. He didn't do it much; in fact, I didn't remember him talking to Dale at all in 1997."

Years later, France said he picked the alias Captain Jack for no special reason. "At the time, it just seemed like a nice name," he said. "It was something to keep people from writing about it." He seemed taken aback that the conversation was public knowledge, and he worried that people might read too much into it. When told that McReynolds had recounted the story on TV, France snapped, "If I'd heard that," he said, "I probably would have come out of my seat."

France's memory and McReynolds' differ on the timing of the brief exchange. France said he likely wouldn't have talked to Earnhardt with the issue still in doubt. McReynolds insists it was under the next-to-last caution, when the Goodwrench Service Plus crew kept their car ahead during its final stop for fuel and tires.

"I remember that day, and I remember talking to Dale under caution," France said. "I wouldn't have ever talked to him or anyone else under green. I called him under that last caution to congratulate him on winning the 500. The only time we ever talk to anyone is after the race, on the cool-down lap or when the caution's out and we need to know about track conditions."

McReynolds doesn't recall any post-race exchange. "Of course, everybody was so excited about winning the race that Bill might have come on the radio," he said. "But there's no question that he talked to Dale under caution with about 25 laps to go. That's the only time I remember hearing 'Captain Jack' and 'Sunday Money' mentioned. If they talked after the race, it would have been very briefly."

As for that memorable 500:

"It was one of the biggest wins by anyone in our sport's history, particularly with all the historical data about Dale not being able to win the Daytona 500," France said. "You know, all the bad luck and the things that happened to him. On and on and on, the things that always seemed to get him. It was an important win for him and for NASCAR."

After years of frustrating heartbreak, Earnhardt won the 500 in dominating fashion. He led 107 of the 200 laps, including the final 61. The key moment—for him, anyway—came when he maintained his tenuous lead while stopping for fuel and right-side tires under caution at lap 174. He drove masterfully down the stretch, fighting off challenges from Bobby Labonte, Jeremy Mayfield, and Rusty Wallace. Jeff Gordon was a serious challenger until fading late with engine problems.

"I was doing a lot of mirror driving," Earnhardt said afterward. "I was gonna get as wide as I had to, but there's only so much you can do when they're coming to you from both sides. I could have held off one, but probably not four. I was fortunate they got to racing each other. I kept working to keep my car in front until somebody turned me over or until we got to the finish line."

He was leading Labonte and Mayfield through Turn 3 on the next-to-last lap, the issue still somewhat in doubt. The laps-down car of Rick Mast was to the inside, and Earnhardt used it to block Labonte and Mayfield, who were racing two-wide for second. When John Andretti and Lake Speed spun on the backstretch, the yellow and white flags effectively froze the field and settled the issue.

The top-10: Earnhardt, Labonte, Mayfield, Ken Schrader, Wallace, Ernie Irvan, Chad Little, Mike Skinner, Michael Waltrip, and Bill Elliott. The 71st of Earnhardt's 76 career victories snapped a 59-race losing streak, dating from March 1996 at Hampton, Georgia. It would be his only victory during an otherwise disappointing season where he finished eighth in points, but nothing would ever take away from that magic moment.

"Dale was about as happy that day as I ever saw him," said Danny "Chocolate" Myers, longtime member of the Childress-owned No. 3 team. "He had a lot

The March 1997 race at Atlanta marked exactly one year since Earnhardt's last victory. Never known as a hot-lap qualifier, Earnhardt's struggles with the clock increased in 1997, and his 26th grid spot at Atlanta was typical. Here, he runs mid-pack, just ahead of Dick Trickle and Michael Waltrip. *Nigel Kinrade*

THE LARRY McREYNOLDS ERA 1997

As the losing streak passed 30—the worst of Dale's career up to that time—fans and admirers sent messages of luck and reassurance. Taped to a crossbar at Talladega in April was a message promising Earnhardt guidance from a guardian angel. "S" is Darrell Waltrip's wife, Stevie. *Nigel Kinrade*

The flat mile at Loudon never quite seemed to suit Earnhardt's restless racing style. Yet, he had one of his best runs ever there in July 1997, and finished a distant second to rising star Jeff Burton. Earnhardt finished more than five seconds behind Burton and did not lead a lap. *Nigel Kinrade*

Earnhardt veers through the chicane at the Watkins Glen course on a beautiful August afternoon. Earnhardt's absolute mastery of ovals, big and small, often overshadowed his road-racing skills, which he illustrated with a victory at Sears Point in 1993, and with his quick grip on sports car racing at Daytona near the end of his life. *Nigel Kinrade*

Crew chief Larry McReynolds, always willing to outwork a team of mules, tries to find out what's wrong after practice at Richmond in September. Nothing went quite right: Earnhardt qualified 22nd, finished out of sight in 15th, and stood fifth in points, 600 behind leader Jeff Gordon. *Nigel Kinrade*

of reasons to smile through the years—the race wins and the championships and all that—but the 500 was a big, big deal for him. It was big for the rest of us, too, but we were more businesslike about it. We loaded up and went home that night because we had a race to run the next weekend.

"I started driving home, but only got to Jacksonville when I had to stop. I was just too tired and too excited to keep going. Besides, I couldn't wait to tell somebody out on the road that we'd just won the Daytona 500, so I told the motel clerk. That was pretty cool, believe me."

Longtime business partner Don Hawk had been close by for many of Earnhardt's greatest moments. He saw his friend revel in his sixth and seventh Winston Cups. He saw 1995 Brickyard 400 victory. He saw many of Earnhardt's last-lap, last-turn, last-shot IROC

Earnhardt was out of the championship's reach by the time of the Phoenix race in November 1997, but he nevertheless cooked up a third-place finish, one of his better results of the second half. Here, Ken Schrader gives Earnhardt plenty of room as Dale makes the pass for third late in the race. Bobby Labonte and Johnny Benson trail. *Nigel Kinrade*

Car owner Richard Childress (left) and crew chief Larry McReynolds talk at Atlanta, the last race of the season. McReynolds' ill-starred tenure peaked in Earnhardt's one and only Daytona 500 victory early the next year, but four months later, McReynolds was transferred to Mike Skinner's companion team, Kevin Hamlin became Earnhardt's handler. *Nigel Kinrade*

miracles, and his mastery of short tracks. What Hawk saw that Sunday night will remain a special memory.

"I'd never seen Dale happier or more excited," he said several years later. "He had been excited about his seventh championship, but that didn't mean as much as winning the Daytona 500. At the end of the victory lane interviews and the press stuff and Sports Center, he was physically and emotionally spent. There wasn't anything left, no energy for a party. He and Teresa just slipped off to their boat. He'd had some wine and champagne, and had smoked a really fine Cuban cigar that got him a little woozy."

Hawk felt confident then, still does, and that Earnhardt was comfortable with his career and didn't need a 500 to certify his legend. "He wanted it," Hawk quickly added, "but I'm convinced he was absolutely, positively satisfied with his life in racing.

Earnhardt, always a 5 o'clock riser, went hard at it from dawn to midnight, and took his rest where he found it. Anyone who worked with Earnhardt any length of time learned to deal with his catnaps. At the end of a difficult year, Earnhardt claims some quiet time at Atlanta. *Nigel Kinrade*

He wouldn't have felt one bit less a driver if hadn't won the 500. He'd proved himself enough so that everybody knew how good he was. He didn't lose any sleep over not having won the 500, then he probably didn't sleep much the night after he finally won it."

At the time, the post-race celebration struck everyone as resembling an assembly of dignitaries lining up to greet visiting royalty. Only later did they realize exactly how right they were. For perhaps the first time in NASCAR history, virtually every crewman from every team queued up like obedient servants to congratulate Earnhardt on finally winning the 500.

The line-up was limited to neither the crew from the No. 3 Goodwrench Service team, the No. 31 Lowe's Home Improvement Warehouse crew of Earnhardt's teammate, Mike Skinner, nor the crew from the No. 1 car of Steve Park, in his first Winston Cup season for Dale Earnhardt Inc.

The receiving line stretched from the Turn 4 end of pit road beyond its midpoint, past the opening where Earnhardt would turn into the Daytona 500's victory lane. The crewmen knew they'd just seen history made, and perhaps more than anyone on the grounds, they could appreciate the significance of the moment.

How many hundreds of times had Earnhardt flashed past these grandstands during his 20 Daytona 500s? On an overcast February afternoon in 1998, Earnhardt—four-time bridesmaid and snakebitten victim several other times— finally won the won race that he, above all others on earth, deserved to win. *Nigel Kinrade*

Earnhardt led 107 of the 200 laps, including the final 61, at the 1998 Daytona 500. Here, he paces Ernie Irvan (36) and Rusty Wallace (2) on the inside rail, while Ken Schrader (33), Mike Skinner (31), and Bobby Labonte (18) bring up the outside. *Nigel Kinrade*

"I sort of expected a few of them to come out there," Earnhardt said of the welcoming committee. "But, man, not as many as there were. So many of the guys came up congratulating me, wanting to shake my hand or give me a high-five or a thumbs-up. I had to go real slow or my arm would have gotten torn off. It really, really means a lot to see how many people were happy for me."

Hawk said Earnhardt often spoke of the moment in reverent terms. "He couldn't believe how many people cared about him," Hawk said. "He was overwhelmed by the show of support. Ex-employees. People he didn't think liked him. People from teams he'd been outrunning for years. It really amazed him they'd stand out there to shake his hand."

Glory be and giant exhale… Earnhardt finally had won himself a Daytona 500. For a man who certainly didn't need anything else to cement his place in history, winning the Great American Race made his resume even more complete. In his 20th try, he grabbed the one brass ring that would mean more than all the rest. His reaction was simple, but eloquent.

Officials, teammates, and fans welcome Earnhardt to the holiest place in stock car racing—victory lane at Daytona. Earnhardt didn't need directions to ground zero. In all the events that are held at Daytona—Busch, IROC, Shootouts, and Twins—Earnhardt won a record 34 times. *Nigel Kinrade*

The inexpressible joy of great achievement glows on Earnhardt's face as he and wife Teresa (left) celebrate. After all of the hard work and heartbreak, Dale closed the loop on the greatest racing career in modern times and finally answered the question, "When you gonna win the 500?" *Nigel Kinrade*

"The Daytona 500 tops them all, buddy. It's the icing on the cake."

The victory brought an end to the longstanding jokes about Earnhardt being good enough to win everything except the Daytona 500.

Example 1: A longtime fan taught his dog to roll over each time Earnhardt was top-10 in the 500 and do back-flips each time he was top-five. When an unsuspecting neighbor asked what the dog did when Earnhardt won the 500, the fan confessed he didn't know.

"After all," he said, "I've only had him 20 years."

Example 2: Another fan found himself staring into a sheet of ice when his lost soul arrived at the gates of Hell. "Son-of-a-gun," he muttered to himself. "Earnhardt musta finally won the 500."

Always, that key word... "finally."

Earnhardt had run his first Winston Cup race at Daytona International Speedway on July 4, 1978. The Firecracker 400 was the first of four superspeedway starts in the No. 96 Ford of team owner Will Cronkite. Not yet an official rookie, Earnhardt started 28th, completed 157 of 160 laps and finished a credible seventh behind David Pearson, Cale Yarborough, Darrell Waltrip, Richard Petty, Lennie Pond, and Dave Marcis. It was the first of his nearly unfathomable 34 top-10 finishes in 46 points races at Daytona Beach.

In fact, Earnhardt finished top-10 in his first 6 DIS starts and in 9 of his first 14. Later, between February 1987 and July 1996, he had an unprecedented string of 18 top-10s in 20 points races. Equally as impressive is this stat: He finished on the lead lap in 17 of them. He was top-10 in six of his last nine DIS starts, and surely was about to finish top-10 the day he crashed and died.

His record at DIS was truly the stuff of legend. He won one Daytona 500 in 23 starts and was top-10 in 16 others. He won two Pepsi Firecracker 400s in 23 starts and was top-10 in 18 others. He won a dozen of the track's 125-mile Daytona 500 qualifying races, including all 10 in the 1990s. He won seven Busch Series 300s, six Budweiser Shootouts, and seven IROC races. His 34 career DIS victories are more than double the 16 of Bobby Allison, second on the track's all-time list.

Earnhardt's characteristic wink-and-grin could confirm a friendship or serve as a warning, depending on the situation. Here, Earnhardt, armed for war at Texas in April, lets a colleague know exactly where things stand. Texas, which opened in 1997, was one of four tracks Earnhardt ran but never conquered. The others were Homestead, New Hampshire, and Watkins Glen. *Nigel Kinrade*

Although not truly a contender in the points race, Earnhardt racked up his best finish since Daytona, a fourth at Martinsville in April. Here, he battles with eventual race winner Bobby Hamilton, who had promised new team owner Larry McClure a short-track victory. Earnhardt stood eighth in points after the run on the Virginia half-mile. *Nigel Kinrade*

If any one moment can possibly erase several heartbreaks (most athletes will say it can't), then the 1998 Daytona 500 was sweet salve for Earnhardt's psyche. NASCAR watchers had almost given up counting the 500s he shoulda, coulda, woulda won... if only.

He'd been second in 1984, third in 1989, second in 1993, second again in 1995, and second yet again in 1996. Earnhardt would be second again in 1999, the year after he finally won it. Who will ever shake the memory of his black-and-silver No. 3 Chevrolet Lumina chattering up the Turn 3 banking on the last lap, slowing abruptly with a flat left-rear tire with the 1990 race, absolutely apparently his.

Love him or hate him—most fans and competitors felt some of both. Almost everyone hoped Earnhardt eventually would win a 500. "He'd been so good for so long down there, you sort of figured the track owed him one," says Richard Petty, a 13-time DIS winner, including a record 7 500s. "If circumstances had been a little different, he would have won three or four 500s. I think the reception he got after winning that [1998] race showed how much people respected him. They might not have always liked him, but they respected what he'd done. I guess some of them felt sorry he'd come so close and not won one before. I think everybody was glad to see it happen."

None was happier than Earnhardt himself. Truth be told, he'd grown weary of hearing the media and fans ask about his chances of ever winning the 500. To his credit, though, he never acted as if it didn't matter. Despite seven championships and 70 career victories, he never hid the fact he wanted his name on the Harley Earl Trophy and his car on display in Daytona USA for a year. When it happened, he reacted appropriately.

"We won it!" he shouted from atop his car in victory lane. Joy spread over his face, his arms were extended skyward, both fists clenched. "We won it!" Then a third time, to match his car number: "We won it!" Moments before, after driving partway along pit road, he'd hung a right and gleefully cut some donuts in the tri-oval grass. Within moments, fans rushed the area to scoop up clumps of grass and stuff them into tote bags. It was NASCAR theater at its best, and few were going to begrudge the winner and his fans their due.

"Twenty years!" he shouted. "Can you believe it? The Daytona 500 is over and we've won it. We've won it. All I can say is that it was my time. Every which way you can lose it, I've lost it. Now, I've won it and I don't care how I won it."

The soft side of Earnhardt emerged on the cool-down lap. He said he didn't exactly cry, but admitted his eyes watered up after taking the yellow and white flags. "Unless something happened to the car, that's when I knew I was going to win it," he said later in a long and emotional press interview. "I was driving slow down the backstretch [coming for the yellow and checkered flags] and I said to myself, 'I want to go fast. I don't want to go slow; I want to get back around there.' So I took off, came back around, took the checkered flag and really got excited."

As Captain Jack certainly agreed… richly deserved excitement.

Earnhardt shows the scars from the previous week at Talladega as he awaits the start of practice at Fontana, California, in May. A violent wreck at the big track, his second there in two years, left Earnhardt with exhaust burns on his face. The fire actually melted his goggles.
Nigel Kinrade

THE
KEVIN HAMLIN ERA

1998–2001

MAKING THE TEAM

By Jonathan Ingram

Page 154: Earnhardt surprised many at the Brickyard in August when he showed up without his trademark mustache. It was the first time he had been clean-shaven since 1982. He shaved the mustache off, he said, because it kept his mask from fitting tightly during a sea-diving trip with Michael Waltrip. Dale finished 10th at Indy and promptly grew the mustache back. *Nigel Kinrade*

In an effort to solve the woes that followed Earnhardt after his 1998 Daytona 500 victory, team owner Richard Childress swapped his team's crew chiefs in early June. He assigned Larry McReynolds to Dale's teammate Mike Skinner and brought Skinner's crew chief, Kevin Hamlin, to Dale's crew. Earnhardt's struggles continued through summer and into fall. At New Hampshire in late August, team manager Bobby Hutchens unloads the back-up car after Earnhardt crashed during practice. Dale held eighth in points for most of the year and could not improve. *Nigel Kinrade*

Whether it was hunting elk on horseback in the mountains of New Mexico or cutting multimillion-dollar business deals, Dale Earnhardt relished new challenges. None was more daunting than joining GM Racing's factory Corvette team for the 24-hour sports car race at Daytona in 2001.

Earnhardt would pilot an unfamiliar, technically advanced car in the unknown territory of the 3.54-mile road course in various conditions during the endurance classic in the opening round of February's Speed Weeks. The glare of publicity that would follow the seven-time stock car champion and one of his co-drivers, son Dale Earnhardt Jr., would magnify any errors.

Already a student of endurance racing, Earnhardt Jr. began practicing on his road-racing video games to prepare himself. Meanwhile, Earnhardt Sr., worried about being on unfamiliar ground, began watching sports car events on TV, where he received the sort of motivation he needed. During the live coverage of the Petit Le Mans at Road Atlanta in October, Andy Pilgrim, driving a factory Corvette, won the race by banging fenders in a high-speed corner with the factory Viper one lap from the finish.

"Two days after that race, I got an overnight letter from Dale," said Pilgrim, who was very impressed by the request of a man he'd never met. Born in England and living in Florida, Pilgrim was asked to become the Winston Cup champion's trail guide for the

THE KEVIN HAMLIN ERA 1998

Page 155: Even though Earnhardt had been mathematically out of the points chase since Rockingham the previous month, he racked up top-11s in the final three races, including eighth place, a lap down, in the inaugural Winston Cup race at Homestead, Florida. *Nigel Kinrade*

Earnhardt returned to the site of his 1998 Daytona triumph and nearly repeated the victory in 1999. Although he never led, he dogged Jeff Gordon for the final 10 laps. Gordon blocked furiously to keep Dale behind him. The 1998 triumph ended a career-longest 59-race losing streak for Dale, but another began immediately and reached 41 before his win at Talladega in April 1999. *Nigel Kinrade*

Corvette program. "Dale said he wouldn't be able to teach me how to rub paint since I already knew about that," said Pilgrim. "But he said he wanted me to teach him how to drive the Corvette."

Earnhardt made a similarly understated but firm approach to the factory team manager Doug Fehan. Expecting a swaggering stock car king, Fehan instead encountered a guy who knew the value of teamwork. "When I first met him, Dale said, 'I know I'm an outsider, but I'm going to work hard to be an insider,'" said Fehan. "He told me he would appreciate it if I treated him just like everybody else on the team."

Although Earnhardt couldn't resist throwing his weight around, albeit very carefully, when he tried to convince Fehan that the driving line-up should be reduced from four to three drivers: himself, Dale Jr., and trusted teacher Pilgrim. That line of thinking lasted only as long as the first full stint during a test session in the Corvette, which had a very hot cockpit due to aerodynamics and a 7.0-liter Chevy V-8 up front. "He got out and he was dripping wet," said Fehan, who had cautioned the stock car driver that shifting and braking would take its toll. "He said, 'I've got to get my ass to the gym. I think that fourth driver is a good idea.'"

What really impressed Fehan and his co-drivers was Earnhardt's decision to fly to the Pratt & Miller shops in Livonia, Michigan, to practice driver changes, a new and important aspect of

road racing for him. Once on the track, the Big E was equally focused on the business at hand and carefully indexed himself up to speed during tests. He also acclimated to the Corvette's vast improvement in braking, acceleration, and downforce, that combined to produce better cornering than a stock car. His biggest worry, Earnhardt told reporters, was "embarrassing myself."

Earnhardt Jr., on the other hand, took to the Corvette C5-R like someone used to road racing in video games, in the words of Fehan, like a rock 'n' roll drummer. At a test in Sebring, Florida, "Dale Jr. immediately tried to go as fast as he could as soon as he got in the car until he crashed," said Fehan. Dale Sr. also had a damaging spin when he carried too much steam into the Sebring course's final turn, a sweeping right-hander. "He knew he had too much speed and jumped on the brakes right away," said Fehan. "He flat-spotted all four tires."

Nervous when out of his usual element, the mild crash in the Corvette was not like bending one of his GM Goodwrench Monte Carlos on a NASCAR oval. "Dale was mortified," said Fehan of the accident. As far as the crew was concerned, Earnhardt was apologetic. "He wasn't just pretending about damaging the car," said Fehan. "He was crying from his soul." The sports car rookie fretted as the team replaced the front nose section damaged in a collision with a tire wall. Then Earnhardt began to brood like a dormant volcano as he watched them. "You could see the determination developing that he was going to master this," said Fehan.

Although there had been plenty of opportunities to practice at night, none of the test days or practices prior to the race had taken place in wet conditions. On race day, clouds threatened overhead, but Earnhardt followed Pilgrim's opening stint in dry conditions. Afterward, Earnhardt was pumped up about driving the 10-turn road circuit amidst the huge field of faster open-cockpit prototypes and slower GT cars. "But I had a hard time keeping the rear tires under it," he said.

The No. 2 Corvette, after the opening stints of Ron Fellows and Johnny O'Connell, pulled out to the lead in the GTS class and ahead of the No. 3 car. Experimental rear suspension pieces

that had been tested, along with new Goodyear tires, helped the No. 2 car's faster laps. The No. 3 Corvette did not enjoy use of the recently developed Goodyears, which Earnhardt knew would cost speed from the outset of the race. During the Daytona test session in January, he would sarcastically remark that he would go home after the 24 Hour and before the Daytona 500 "to pay some Goodyear tire bills." Journalists were otherwise kept completely in the dark about the disparity in the cars and tires until long after the race had been run.

Earnhardt was better than equal, naturally, on the banking portion of the combined infield and oval circuit, where the stock car driver could milk more speed than the sports car specialists. "I was faster than Dale through the infield, but once we got out on the banking, he would pull away from me," said the veteran O'Connell, who diced with Earnhardt for two laps during their opening stints before he drafted past to lap him. "He knew where every bump was on the track."

Rank has its privileges, and Dale Jr. suffered the unkind fate of watching the rain begin to fall shortly before his opening stint, which was fourth in the rotation. Rain-master Pilgrim followed fellow road racer Kelly Collins as the younger Earnhardt was forced to wait. Once the rain continued to fall, Little E got his chance after nightfall on a muddy track. Trying to be too polite for other traffic in the East Horseshoe, he took the muddy inside line after exiting the pits and promptly spun.

Another spin by Earnhardt Jr. did not cost much more time than the different car set-ups. The ultimate dagger in the heart of victory, occurred during the night when an axle

The first third of the season was mystifying, especially in qualifying, with Earnhardt took three provisionals through April. He struggled at Martinsville in the spring, started 39th and struggled to 19th two laps down. Here, he is about to be lapped by Jeff Gordon, who led 255 of the 500 laps and finished third. John Andretti was the winner. *Nigel Kinrade*

Earnhardt's breakthrough came in late April at monstrous Talladega, where he was the undisputed king. He charged from 16th after his final pit stop, passed Dale Jarrett for the lead with 14 to go, and easily led Jarrett to the stripe. The celebration included car owner Richard Childress (left) and wife Teresa. *Nigel Kinrade*

broke. The repair time in the pits left the No. 3 Corvette second in class behind the leading No. 2 Corvette, which, at halfway, was near the top of the leader board with the faster prototypes, despite their furious pace.

Earnhardt took his final turn around dawn on Sunday and was given a lap time to run, a standard strategy. Within a handful of laps, Earnhardt was consistently circulating two seconds faster than the target time—with Pilgrim on the radio headset offering help and

guidance regarding the fastest line in the wet. Pilgrim watched Earnhardt on a monitor via the live Speedvision coverage of the race.

"Dale asked to do a second stint," said Fehan. "I said, Okay. You can go again. Then halfway during the second stint, he came on and said he wanted to go a third time. I said no. He spent the entire second half of that stint talking to me on the radio, trying to let him go a third stint."

"I made him get out," continued Fehan. "But you could tell that he had reached a performance pinnacle. He was capable of driving the Corvette at competitive times in the rain. He had realized that he had succeeded. He was one with the car and had become a Corvette driver. The team wasn't carrying him. He was carrying his own weight."

Earnhardt emerged from the car in the overcast morning in the brightness of his team's pits with blue-gray eyes as big as headlights. "They told me a lap time to do. Shoot, I was two seconds under that in a couple of laps," he said with a big grin. "I need this Corvette and all this downforce when I go up to Watkins Glen for the Winston Cup race."

The evening sun in the Tennessee hills shows on Earnhardt's face as he prepares for the start of the Bristol night race in August and reflects on a difficult season. Earnhardt stood seventh in points, nearly 700 behind leader Dale Jarrett, and started at Bristol in 26th position. *Nigel Kinrade*

Backlit by fireworks in Bristol's fourth-turn victory square, Earnhardt celebrates a controversial victory, his second win of the season. He and Terry Labonte battled through the second half of the race, and Earnhardt spun Labonte out on the last lap to win. "I was just trying to rattle his cage," Earnhardt said innocently. *Nigel Kinrade*

Below: The Moment. Amid the tumult and uproar of a wild night at Bristol in August 1999, Earnhardt and crew enjoy the pure thrill of victory. Earnhardt treats his teammates and colleagues to a champagne spray as the celebration hits high gear. Winning never gets old, and each of Dale's 76 wins was as sweet as all the others. *Nigel Kinrade*

After a second rear axle repair, the No. 3 Corvette went on to a second-place finish in the GTS class, fourth overall behind the No. 2 Corvette, which won the race, as well as its class, after the faster prototypes retired with mechanical failures.

"Dale told me he was having the most fun he'd ever had in racing," said Fehan. In addition to the high-performance capabilities of the Corvette, co-driving with his son had a major impact on Earnhardt, who next wanted to tackle the world's biggest 24-hour race. "One day soon, we're going to find a way in our schedule to get over to Le Mans and see what that's like," Earnhardt told Fehan. "Me and my boys are going to do Le Mans."

The famous French endurance event would be a challenge Earnhardt never tackled. Two weeks after the conclusion of his first 24-hour, a crash on the last lap of the Daytona 500 took his life.

Earnhardt never really was into the race in September at New Hampshire, a tight, flat track where passing is all but impossible. Here, he runs mid-pack, single-file, with Bill Elliott, Jeff Burton, and Mark Martin. Not one of this group led a single lap, and Earnhardt came home 13th. The winner? Joe Nemechek, in Felix Sabates' car. *Nigel Kinrade*

In a classic pastime pose, Earnhardt sits on the asphalt beside his car on pit road, and waits for practice to begin at Charlotte. From there, partly out of sight of the passing crowd, Earnhardt could eye the action up and down the row and do some thinking. *Nigel Kinrade*

TOUGH LOVE

By Jonathan Ingram

When Dale Earnhardt's two sons made their intentions clear about embarking on racing careers, did they get any help from their father, a Winston Cup champion? They received the exact same response Dale received from his father, a NASCAR Late Model Sportsman champion. Come back later, Dale told them, when you've demonstrated that you really want to race.

Kerry and Dale Earnhardt Jr.'s first race car was a street stock entry salvaged from a junkyard after they spent $500 of their own money. They further pooled their assets to enter the car in local short-track events in the Charlotte area and took turns behind the wheel along with their sister Kelly.

Earnhardt's sons eventually excelled well enough to get their father's support to move up to the Late Model Stock division of NASCAR's Winston Racing Series, where they still had to work on their own entry. Dale Jr. showed enough promise to be promoted to the Busch Series in cars owned by Dale Earnhardt Inc. After two Busch Series championships, Dale Jr. moved to the Winston Cup in Dale Earnhardt Inc. entries numbered 8, his grandfather's number.

"Dale made Dale Jr. work on his own cars before he helped him," said David Oliver. "Richard Petty gave his son Kyle a Dodge Magnum to race at Daytona for his first race and he won the ARCA (Automobile Racing Club of America) race, but Dale would never let Dale Jr. do something like that. That comes from Ralph making him make his own way.

"Eventually Dale would have driven for his father," continued Oliver. "Had Ralph lived another year or two, Dale'd have been driving for him on the dirt tracks [instead of pursuing a Winston Cup ride]. Whether his career would have gone as far is anybody's guess. By the fact of losing his father, Dale might have moved right on up to stardom."

In a typical father-son meeting, Earnhardt tries to make a point to Dale Jr., who seems to be trying not to listen. Young Earnhardt, however, caught on quickly, and won seven races and the first of his two Busch Series championships in his first full season in Dad's ACDelco cars. *Nigel Kinrade*

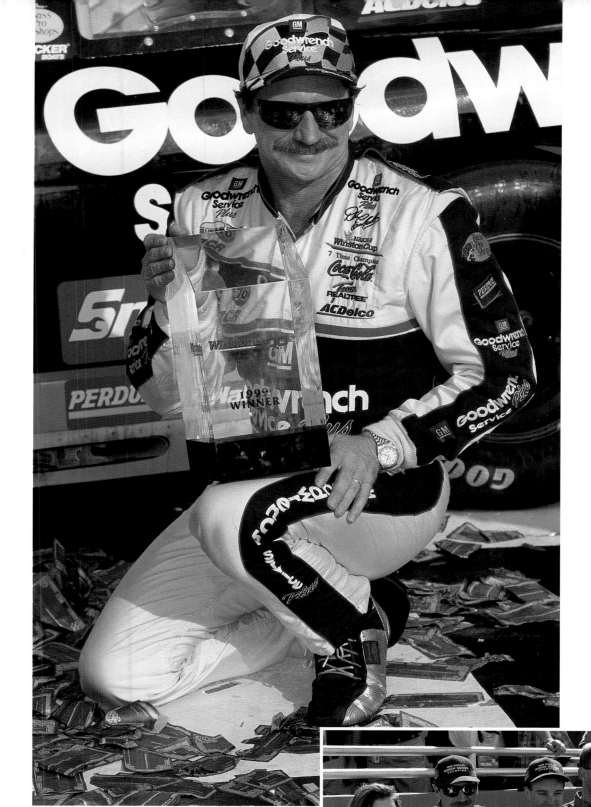

Earnhardt's spotty season hit another high in the fall at Talladega. He again outmaneuvered Dale Jarrett to win at the big track for a season sweep of Talladega. Earnhardt won 10 times in all at the Alabama course, more than twice as often as anyone else. *Nigel Kinrade*

On the bright side at Homestead, Earnhardt and family celebrated the second consecutive Busch Series championship for Dale Jr., who was prepping for the step up to Winston Cup in 2000 aboard Dad's new, Budweiser-sponsored cars. Teresa, Junior's stepmother, shares in the victory. *Nigel Kinrade*

Corporate ties and promotional duties handed Earnhardt a red Chevrolet for the 2000 Daytona 500. The red identity underscored the introduction of Chevy's updated Monte Carlo and its advertising tie-ins with TimeWarner's Tasmanian Devil character. Unfortunately, the Monte was nowhere near up to speed which led to loud and effective complaints from Earnhardt after his 21st-place finish. *Nigel Kinrade*

By the time of the season's first "aero" race at Atlanta in March, NASCAR had granted the Chevrolets their infamous 2-inch kick-out on the front valance, a variance that was hotly disputed by the Ford teams. Earnhardt immediately cashed in and won the Atlanta race, albeit barely a bumper ahead of charging Bobby Labonte. The Chevy change, and the subsequent Atlanta result, emphasized Earnhardt's influence among NASCAR's top brass. *Nigel Kinrade*

Richard Childress remained the one adult male Dale would yield to when it came to nails and tacks. Although Earnhardt and Childress had their disputes over their 18 years and six championships, there was a kinship between driver and owner that went to depths only the two men knew—a relationship that has yet to be duplicated in the sport. Here, Childress and Earnhardt confer at Bristol in late March. *Nigel Kinrade*

Martinsville Speedway, NASCAR's oldest track, always presents a challenge. The reconfigured single pit road (the speedway had front and back pits for its first 50 years) created an impossibly tight work space for Earnhardt and crew in the 2000 spring race. Earnhardt won six times at Martinsville. He's fourth on the Virginia track's all-time list. Earnhardt finished 17, on the lead lap, in the caution-filled April race. *Nigel Kinrade*

THE MAYFIELD FACTOR

By Jonathan Ingram

For many years, Ray Cooper worked as the public relations representative for Chevrolet in the Winston Cup. It didn't take him long to notice that Dale Earnhardt hated losing. If the perennial champ did not win a race, he immediately started a new competition that he was determined to win—the race to leave the track.

"If he didn't go to victory lane, you always had to try to get to Earnhardt first if you were going to get any quotes," said Cooper. "There were some races where he went right from the race car and stepped into a waiting van and left the track."

The strangest post-race interview Cooper had with Earnhardt occurred in Atlanta after the final race of the 2000 season when Earnhardt finished second in points to Bobby Labonte. The driver of the GM Goodwrench Chevy also finished second that day in the race to Jerry Nadeau. As Cooper walked hurriedly through the garage with Earnhardt to get his comments, the seven-time champion referred constantly to the race winner as Jeremy Mayfield, not Jerry Nadeau.

This was strange, since Mayfield had left after 53 laps with a blown engine. "He kept saying 'Mayfield' where he meant to say 'Nadeau,'" said Cooper. "Finally, I said to him, 'Dale, you know Jerry Nadeau won the race, don't you?' He said, 'Yeah, yeah, I meant Nadeau.'"

The incident clearly indicated Earnhardt's preoccupation with a race earlier in the year, when Mayfield knocked him out of the lead in the last corner at Pocono. Instead of a third victory and

Sign language occasionally got Dale's point across more succintly than words. *Brian Cleary*

being within 42 points of Labonte in the championship after just 15 races, Earnhardt finished fourth in the race, which was rather shameful for a guy known as "The Intimidator."

Earnhardt figured Mayfield had cost his Kevin Hamlin-led team much-needed momentum in the championship. He made a public show of his response to Mayfield with a single finger salute after the race and then, two races later, he pinched Mayfield on the neck and reminded the Kentuckian that he could expect the usual discipline for such behavior in the Winston Cup. "Paybacks are hell, boy," he told Mayfield during the drivers' meeting in Daytona that summer, as if to warn other drivers as well.

What really cost Earnhardt his last shot at the championship that year was a series of three races where he lost 172 points to Labonte. He blew a tire at Pocono, Pennsylvania—most likely due to an aggressive chassis set-up. After starting and finishing eighth at the Brickyard 400 (a race which Labonte won), an unforced error spun Earnhardt on the first lap at Watkins Glen, New York.

Earnhardt finished his last full season 13th in miles led and was in front for only 11 events, compared to 23 by Labonte, who was tops that year in the Winston Cup. With two victories, including his incredible 17th-to-first-place run in the final four laps at Talladega, Alabama, Earnhardt, was second in miles completed, and once again had worked his old reliable formula of consistency.

Labonte, in fact, had adopted the Earnhardt formula himself, and finished all but 13 miles. The Texan led relatively few miles in the 23 races where he was in front. He finished with four victories, second to Tony Stewart's six, reminiscent of Earnhardt finishing behind Rusty Wallace in victories during his last two championships.

Determined to win an eighth Winston Cup, Earnhardt, at age 49, worked his familiar formula in the Daytona 500 in 2001, and ran aggressively to set the tone for the coming championship chase. After all, he had never won the Daytona 500 in any of the years he had won the championship, so the important thing was to come out of Speed Weeks with momentum.

As the laps wound down, so a broken front air dam prevented him from leading, so the third-placed Earnhardt fought to help the Dale Earnhardt Inc. cars of Michael Waltrip and Dale Earnhardt Jr., first and second. Earnhardt, often known for trying to do too many things at once, also was trying to maintain his reputation as a tough guy to pass by single-handedly trying to hold off Sterling Marlin, Ken Schrader, and Wallace, when his fatal accident occurred in Turn 4 on the final lap.

Another freakish "special" was unveiled at The Winston at Charlotte in May 2000. GM Parts commissioned artist Peter Max to create a paint job for both The Winston and the Coca-Cola 600. Max's rainbow effects kindled unwelcome comparisons to Jeff Gordon's Rainbow Warriors. Even Earnhardt drew comparisons to his first sportsman car, the pink-and-apricot metal flake car at Concord Speedway. To rugged veteran Chocolate Meyers (seen here), a race car's a race car. *Nigel Kinrade*

Earnhardt was seldom outwardly emotional. He gave and accepted affection on his own terms. This was even true in his relationship with second son Dale Jr., who had earned his father's racing graces with two Busch Series championships in Dad's cars. Junior graduated to Winston Cup in 2000, won twice, and just missed rookie-of-the-year. Here, Junior follows Dale's footsteps at Dover in June. *Nigel Kinrade*

Dale's relationship with his racing son was almost equal to his relationship with his motorsport baby, Dale Earnhardt Inc. DEI was hatched from Earnhardt's long-lived Busch effort with Long Islander Steve Park. Park won Busch rookie-of-the-year for Earnhardt in 1997 and moved up to Cup full-time in 1998. The Park Promise came to fruition at the Watkins Glen road course in August 2000, when Steve earned his first Cup victory. *Nigel Kinrade*

Earnhardt counsels Dale Jr. at Darlington in September. Junior, in a high-pressure rookie year with sponsor Budweiser, above all needed to learn the pace of a 34-race season, and faded somewhat after a fast start. He lost the rookie-of-the-year award to Matt Kenseth. *Brian Cleary*

The New Hampshire race in September was a salvage operation, and Earnhardt finished 12th, a lap down, after he started 37th. By mid-September, points are critical, and Earnhardt tried to keep pace with runaway leader Bobby Labonte, but he fell from second to fourth in the standings after the New Hampshire finish. Dale eventually regained second place, but finished 265 points back. *Nigel Kinrade*

The greatest masterpiece of Earnhardt's career came at Talladega in October 2000. Although trapped in 18th place with five laps to go, he coolly drove to the front with two laps remaining, and demonstrated his mastery of the most difficult conditions NASCAR can offer, restrictor-plate racing. After Earnhardt's fantastic drive, the stands at Talladega roared for a full five minutes in tribute to one of the greatest drives in racing history. *Nigel Kinrade*

The champagne and trophy were almost afterthoughts in Talladega's victory lane, as Earnhardt fully realized he had done the impossible and had put on a show for all time. This was perhaps the greatest of all the stunning achievements that set Earnhardt apart from the congregation. No matter what else happened, Earnhardt, at 49, had left motorsports with an unimpeachable memory. *Nigel Kinrade*

　　　THE KEVIN HAMLIN ERA 2000

Confident and relaxed on the Thursday before the 2001 Daytona 500 qualifying heats, Earnhardt shares a laugh with old buddy Dave Marcis. Through the Thursday races (Dale finished sixth in the second 125), Earnhardt had not won anything during Speed Weeks for the first time since 1989. His three DEI cars, driven by Michael Waltrip, Dale Jr., and Steve Park, were serious contenders, and his No. 3 was good enough to drive Daytona. *Nigel Kinrade*

During driver introductions, Earnhardt gives an animated lecture to Tony Stewart (left), Dale Jr. (foreground), and Rusty Wallace (right). As usual when the master spoke, everyone else listened. Junior finished second in the 500 and Wallace third. Stewart was caught in the 18-car wreck on Lap 178 and didn't finish. *Nigel Kinrade*

Earnhardt and Mike Skinner had been teammates since 1997, when owner Richard Childress drafted the Truck Series champ and expanded to two teams. During that time span, Skinner won the Daytona 500 pole in 1997 and a qualifying heat in 2001. Skinner's car was damaged in the Lap 178 wreck, but he managed to limp home after repairs. *Nigel Kinrade*

Earnhardt, as always, received commendable pit work all day. During the stops that followed the big wreck, the RCR team got Earnhardt in and out in fourth place. On the restart, Dale and Rusty Wallace drafted by Ricky Rudd, and Earnhardt took third behind Michael Waltrip and Dale Jr. Earnhardt was in third when the events unfolded in

History in the Making. Earnhardt, the champion, leads Robby Gordon (4) and Steve Park (1) on the outside as the draft heats up. Bobby Hamilton (55) and Jason Leffler (01) pace the inside row. In the middle is Michael Waltrip, driving his first race in Earnhardt's No. 15. Although caught in a bad spot, Waltrip had shown superior skill in restricted races, and it paid off that Sunday for Waltrip and DEI. *Nigel Kinrade*

From the time of Jeff Gordon's arrival in 1993, he had been linked in destiny with Earnhardt. Earnhardt won his sixth championship in 1993 and his seventh in 1994. Gordon dominated the rest of the decade and won the season trophies in 1995, 1997, and 1998. The two heroes were very different men, yet in competition they always showed each other the highest respect. *Nigel Kinrade*

THE KEVIN HAMLIN ERA 2001

In one of the last photographs of the American hero, Earnhardt prepares for his final race, the 2001 Daytona 500. Earnhardt's career and life ended in the last turn of the last lap of the first race of the twenty-first century. *Brian Cleary*

The reality of Earnhardt's death had begun to sink in as fans and competitors traveled to Rockingham, North Carolina, in the week that followed. The Rock, where Earnhardt had won three times, was a somber place. The mood was darkened further by nagging rain. Countless tributes and expressions of grief and remembrance cluttered the front entrance to the rural speedway, two hours from Earnhardt's home. *Nigel Kinrade*

Five months after Earnhardt's death, tributes and testimonials continued undiminished. One of the most touching and spontaneous was the Goodwrench souvenir rig, on which literally tens of thousands of fans wrote short dedications to their hero. By midseason, the trailer (shown here at Pocono) was completely covered with script. Fans stood on one another's shoulders to reach the last untouched spots. *Nigel Kinrade*

APPENDIX

Dale Earnhardt's Winston Cup Record

Year	Race	Finish	Start	Laps Completed	Condition	Money
1975	Charlotte–World 600	22	33	355	Running	2,425
1976	Charlotte–World 600	31	25	156	DNF–Engine	1,725
	Atlanta–Dixie 500	19	16	260	DNF–Crash	1,360
1977	Charlotte–NAPA National 500	38	36	25	DNF–Mechanical	1,375
1978	Charlotte–World 600	17	28	382	Running	3,415
	Daytona–Firecracker 400	7	28	157	Running	3,990
	Talladega–Talladega 500	12	27	180	Running	2,740
	Darlington–Southern 500	16	14	313	Running	3,100
	Atlanta–Dixie 500	4	10	327	Running	7,500
1979	Riverside–Winston Western 500	21	10	103	Running	2,230
	Daytona–Daytona 500	8	10	199	Running	22,845
	Rockingham–Carolina 500	12	5	460	Running	3,250
	Richmond–Richmond 400	13	4	390	Running	2,015
	Atlanta–Atlanta 500	12	17	321	Running	4,835
	North Wilkesboro–Northwestern Bank 400	4	5	400	Running	4,275
	Bristol–Southeastern 500	1	9	500	Running	19,800
	Darlington–CRC Chemicals Rebel 500	23	13	300	Running	5,600
	Martinsville–Virginia 500	8	11	495	Running	4,200
	Talladega–Winston 500	36	14	4	DNF–Crash	5,075
	Nashville–Sun-Drop Music City USA 420	4	7	419	Running	5,350
	Dover–Mason-Dixon 500	5	6	497	Running	7,750
	Charlotte–World 600	3	15	400	Running	27,100
	Texas World–Texas 400	12	3	189	DNF–Crash	6,400
	Riverside–NAPA Riverside 400	13	1	87	Running	7,250
	Michigan–Gabriel 400	6	13	200	Running	7,540
	Daytona–Firecracker 400	3	21	160	Running	14,980
	Nashville–Busch Nashville 420	3	3	417	Running	7,200
	Pocono–Coca-Cola 500	29	3	98	DNF–Crash	4,680
	Talladega–Talladega 500	Did Not Start Due to Injury				
	Michigan–Champion Spark Plug 400	Did Not Start Due to Injury				
	Bristol–Volunteer 500	Did Not Start Due to Injury				
	Darlington–Southern 500	Did Not Start Due to Injury				
	Richmond–Capital City 400	4	1	399	Running	7,250
	Dover–CRC Chemicals 500	9	1	495	Running	7,000
	Martinsville–Old Dominion 500	29	5	67	DNF–Crash	3,510
	Charlotte–NAPA National 500	10	8	327	Running	14,515
	North Wilkesboro–Holly Farms 400	4	1	398	Running	10,425
	Rockingham–American 500	5	10	488	Running	8,300
	Atlanta–Dixie 500	2	7	328	Running	16,700
	Ontario–Los Angeles Times 500	9	6	199	Running	7,500
1980	Riverside–Winston Western 500	2	5	119	Running	19,400
	Daytona–Daytona 500	4	32	199	Running	36,350
	Richmond–Richmond 400	5	13	398	Running	6,550
	Rockingham–Carolina 500	3	7	491	Running	14,420
	Atlanta–Atlanta 500	1	31	328	Running	36,200
	Bristol–Valleydale Southeastern 500	1	4	500	Running	20,625
	Darlington–CRC Chemicals Rebel 500	29	5	104	DNF–Engine	6,640
	North Wilkesboro–Northwestern Bank 400	6	4	395	Running	6,525
	Martinsville–Virginia 500	13	11	484	Running	5,400
	Talladega–Winston 500	2	4	188	Running	28,700
	Nashville–Music City USA 420	6	7	418	Running	5,825
	Dover–Mason-Dixon 500	10	16	475	DNF–Engine	7,675
	Charlotte–World 600	20	4	367	Running	13,690
	Texas World–NASCAR 400	9	7	191	Running	8,800
	Riverside–Warner W. Hodgdon 400	5	5	95	Running	9,100
	Michigan–Gabriel 400	12	3	197	Running	7,825
	Daytona–Firecracker 400	3	7	160	Running	16,580
	Nashville–Busch Nashville 420	1	7	420	Running	14,600
	Pocono–Coca-Cola 500	4	11	200	Running	11,415
	Talladega–Talladega 500	3	16	188	Running	16,975
	Michigan–Champion Spark Plug 400	35	8	79	DNF–Engine	6,410
	Bristol–Busch Volunteer 500	2	7	500	Running	11,450
	Darlington–Southern 500	7	8	366	Running	11,125

Year	Race	Finish	Start	Laps Completed	Condition	Money
	Richmond–Capital City 400	4	5	399	Running	7,575
	Dover–CRC Chemicals 500	34	9	151	DNF–Engine	6,210
	North Wilkesboro–Holly Farms 400	5	8	399	Running	6,925
	Martinsville–Old Dominion 500	1	7	500	Running	25,375
	Charlotte–National 500	1	4	334	Running	49,050
	Rockingham–American 500	18	11	443	Running	6,650
	Atlanta–Atlanta Journal 500	3	13	327	Running	14,700
	Ontario–Los Angeles Times 500	5	2	200	Running	10,835
1981	Riverside–Winston Western 500	3	6	119	Running	16,325
	Daytona–Daytona 500	5	7	200	Running	37,365
	Richmond–Richmond 400	7	6	397	Running	7,550
	Rockingham–Carolina 500	26	11	285	DNF–Crash	8,250
	Atlanta–Coca-Cola 500	3	5	327	Running	19,400
	Bristol–Valleydale 500	28	2	140	DNF–Crash	7,270
	North Wilkesboro–Northwestern Bank 400	10	2	395	Running	8,800
	Darlington–CRC Chemicals Rebel 500	17	5	346	Running	9,150
	Martinsville–Virginia 500	25	10	155	DNF–Engine	6,600
	Talladega–Winston 500	8	4	183	Running	14,775
	Nashville–Melling Tool 420	20	12	379	Running	6,500
	Dover–Mason-Dixon 500	3	14	499	Running	15,125
	Charlotte–World 600	18	5	362	DNF–Engine	13,675
	Texas World–Budweiser NASCAR 400	2	3	200	Running	18,650
	Riverside–Warner W. Hodgdon 400	2	2	95	Running	18,725
	Michigan–Gabriel 400	5	7	200	Running	11,925
	Daytona–Firecracker 4002	35	3	71	DNF–Mechanical	8,360
	Nashville–Busch Nashville 420	7	7	418	Running	7,375
	Pocono–Mountain Dew 500	11	8	198	Running	9,190
	Talladega–Talladega 500	29	3	83	DNF–Mechanical	9,375
	Michigan–Champion Spark Plug 400	9	10	200	Running	7,955
	Bristol–Busch 500	27	14	31	DNF–Crash	2,620
	Darlington–Southern 500	6	10	366	Running	10,695
	Richmond–Wrangler Sanfor-Set 400	6	11	398	Running	6,270
	Dover–CRC Chemicals 500	15	22	490	Running	5,275
	Martinsville–Old Dominion 500	26	7	148	DNF–Engine	2,690
	North Wilkesboro–Holly Farms 400	4	10	399	Running	7,270
	Charlotte–National 500	25	24	220	DNF–Mechanical	4,920
	Rockingham–American 500	9	5	489	Running	7,360
	Atlanta–Atlanta Journal 500	25	9	222	DNF–Engine	4,290
	Riverside–Winston Western 500	4	3	119	Running	10,560
1982	Daytona–Daytona 500	36	10	44	DNF–Engine	14,700
	Richmond–Richmond 400	4	8	250	Running	10,960
	Bristol–Valleydale 500	2	9	500	Running	18,480
	Atlanta–Coca-Cola 500	28	1	211	DNF–Engine	21,375
	Rockingham–Warner W. Hodgdon Carolina 500	25	6	191	DNF–Mechanical	8,660
	Darlington–CRC Chemicals Rebel 500	1	5	367	Running	31,450
	North Wilkesboro–Northwestern Bank 400	3	14	400	Running	12,425
	Martinsville–Virginia National Bank 500	23	15	100	DNF–Mechanical	7,170
	Talladega–Winston 500	8	20	186	Running	14,850
	Nashville–Cracker Barrel 420	10	12	415	Running	7,735
	Dover–Mason-Dixon 500	3	10	497	Running	15,700
	Charlotte–World 600	30	15	279	DNF–Mechanical	18,470
	Pocono–Van Scoy Diamond Mine 500	34	4	45	DNF–Mechanical	8,575
	Riverside–Budweiser 400	4	5	95	Running	11,935
	Michigan–Gabriel 400	7	11	199	Running	13,550
	Daytona–Firecracker 400	29	13	89	DNF–Engine	9,265
	Nashville–Busch Nashville 420	9	13	417	Running	7,635
	Pocono–Mountain Dew 500	25	7	134	DNF–Crash	9,700
	Talladega–Talladega 500	35	18	29	DNF–Crash	9,290
	Michigan–Champion Spark Plug 400	30	18	76	DNF–Mechanical	8,750
	Bristol–Busch 500	6	12	499	Running	9,600
	Darlington–Southern 500	3	5	367	Running	21,225
	Richmond–Wrangler Sanfor-Set 400	27	6	158	DNF–Engine	7,105
	Dover–CRC Chemicals 500	20	16	402	DNF–Mechanical	8,825
	North Wilkesboro–Holly Farms 400	20	15	365	DNF–Mechanical	7,235
	Charlotte–National 500	25	15	237	DNF–Mechanical	9,565
	Martinsville–Old Dominion 500	27	12	118	DNF–Mechanical	7,230
	Rockingham–Warner W. Hodgdon American 500	14	8	445	DNF–Engine	9,300

Year	Race	Finish	Start	Laps Completed	Condition	Money
	Atlanta–Atlanta Journal 500	34	8	85	DNF–Crash	8,385
	Riverside–Winston Western 500	42	7	8	DNF–Mechanical	8,125
1983	Daytona–Daytona 500	35	3	63	DNF–Engine	37,011
	Richmond–Richmond 400	2	8	400	Running	16,575
	Rockingham–Warner W. Hodgdon Carolina 500	33	4	73	DNF–Crash	8,000
	Atlanta–Coca-Cola 500	33	8	246	DNF–Engine	8,075
	Darlington–TranSouth 500	13	17	348	DNF–Engine	7,890
	North Wilkesboro–Northwestern Bank 400	29	11	40	DNF–Engine	6,450
	Martinsville–Virginia National Bank 500	26	11	351	DNF–Crash	7,240
	Talladega–Winston 500	24	17	120	DNF–Mechanical	10,035
	Nashville–Marty Robbins 420	24	7	258	DNF–Engine	6,450
	Dover–Mason-Dixon 500	8	17	491	Running	10,500
	Bristol–Valleydale 500	9	5	495	Running	7,930
	Charlotte–World 600	5	3	399	Running	28,700
	Riverside–Budweiser 400	4	15	95	Running	11,475
	Pocono–Van Scoy Diamond Mine 500	8	9	199	Running	11,200
	Michigan–Gabriel 400	15	15	198	Running	10,125
	Daytona–Firecracker 400	9	7	158	Running	11,900
	Nashville–Busch Nashville 420	1	3	420	Running	23,125
	Pocono–Like Cola 500	30	10	71	DNF–Engine	8,500
	Talladega–Talladega 500	1	4	188	Running	46,950
	Michigan–Champion Spark Plug 400	7	13	200	Running	12,140
	Bristol–Busch 500	2	6	419	Running	15,725
	Darlington–Southern 500	11	17	363	Running	11,855
	Richmond–Wrangler Sanfor-Set 400	22	9	181	DNF–Mechanical	6,850
	Dover–Budweiser 5001	35	3	90	DNF–Mechanical	7,890
	Martinsville–Goody's 500	4	5	499	Running	11,200
	North Wilkesboro–Holly Farms 400	2	6	400	Running	15,500
	Charlotte–Miller High Life 500	14	16	332	Running	11,650
	Rockingham–Warner W. Hodgdon American 500	17	16	436	DNF–Engine	9,330
	Atlanta–Atlanta Journal 500	33	2	49	DNF–Mechanical	7,995
	Riverside–Winston Western 500	4	9	119	Running	13,725
1984	Daytona–Daytona 500	2	29	200	Running	81,825
	Richmond–Miller High Life 400	6	17	399	Running	8,675
	Rockingham–Warner W. Hodgdon Carolina 500	14	8	470	Running	9,335
	Atlanta–Coca-Cola 500	2	9	328	Running	26,935
	Bristol–Valleydale 500	7	17	498	Running	7,530
	North Wilkesboro–Northwestern Bank 400	8	10	399	Running	7,260
	Darlington–TranSouth 500	5	14	366	Running	12,825
	Martinsville–Sovran Bank 500	9	15	497	Running	7,345
	Talladega–Winston 500	27	5	149	Running	10,475
	Nashville–Coors 420	19	5	410	Running	7,250
	Dover–Budweiser 500	5	11	499	Running	11,600
	Charlotte–World 600	2	19	400	Running	49,625
	Riverside–Budweiser 400	5	3	95	Running	10,950
	Pocono–Van Scoy Diamond Mine 500	8	8	199	Running	11,360
	Michigan–Miller High Life 400	2	15	200	Running	28,175
	Daytona–Pepsi Firecracker 400	8	2	159	Running	13,600
	Nashville–Pepsi 420	3	16	419	Running	10,775
	Pocono–Like Cola 500	10	5	198	Running	11,300
	Talladega–Talladega 500	1	3	188	Running	47,100
	Michigan–Champion Spark Plug 400	7	14	199	Running	12,700
	Bristol–Busch 500	10	9	478	Running	7,800
	Darlington–Southern 500	38	20	57	DNF–Engine	7,860
	Richmond–Wrangler Sanfor-Set 400	3	13	400	Running	13,450
	Dover–Delaware 500	5	2	497	Running	11,710
	Martinsville–Goody's 500	12	11	489	Running	7,865
	Charlotte–Miller High Life 500	39	16	74	DNF–Engine	8,010
	North Wilkesboro–Holly Farms 400	7	9	400	Running	8,150
	Rockingham–Warner W. Hodgdon American 500	13	6	470	Running	8,710
	Atlanta–Atlanta Journal 500	1	10	328	Running	40,610
	Riverside–Winston Western 500	11	4	119	Running	9,000
1985	Daytona–Daytona 500	32	18	84	DNF–Engine	17,150
	Richmond–Miller High Life 400	1	4	400	Running	33,625
	Rockingham–Carolina 500	10	11	491	Running	16,300
	Atlanta–Coca-Cola 500	9	8	326	Running	12,125
	Bristol–Valleydale 500	1	12	500	Running	31,525
	Darlington–TranSouth 500	24	8	293	DNF–Engine	9,180

Year	Race	Finish	Start	Laps Completed	Condition	Money
	North Wilkesboro–Northwestern Bank 400	8	8	398	Running	8,340
	Martinsville–Sovran Bank 500	25	4	345	DNF–Engine	8,975
	Talladega–Winston 500	21	13	155	DNF–Engine	11,410
	Dover–Budweiser 500	25	9	219	DNF–Engine	9,050
	Charlotte–Coca-Cola World 600	4	5	399	Running	49,238
	Riverside–Budweiser 400	40	13	19	DNF–Engine	8,240
	Pocono–Van Scoy Diamond Mine 500	39	4	3	DNF–Engine	8,700
	Michigan–Miller 400	5	14	200	Running	17,925
	Daytona–Pepsi Firecracker 400	9	18	159	Running	13,400
	Pocono–Summer 500	39	11	11	DNF–Engine	8,700
	Talladega–Talladega 500	24	14	156	Running	11,080
	Michigan–Champion Spark Plug 400	22	12	191	Running	9,525
	Bristol–Busch 500	1	1	500	Running	34,675
	Darlington–Southern 500	19	5	349	DNF–Engine	12,835
	Richmond–Wrangler Sanfor-Set 400	4	9	400	Running	12,050
	Dover–Delaware 500	7	8	496	Running	12,600
	Martinsville–Goody's 500	1	11	500	Running	37,725
	North Wilkesboro–Holly Farms 400	4	7	400	Running	10,960
	Charlotte–Miller High Life 500	20	5	301	Running	12,050
	Rockingham–Nationwise 500	8	15	489	Running	11,800
	Atlanta–Atlanta Journal 500	4	13	328	Running	15,300
	Riverside–Winston Western 500	5	7	119	Running	13,175
1986	Daytona–Daytona 500	14	4	197	DNF–Engine	61,655
	Richmond–Miller High Life 400	3	10	400	Running	19,310
	Rockingham–Goodwrench 500	8	5	490	Running	19,510
	Atlanta–Motorcraft 500	2	1	328	Running	51,300
	Bristol–Valleydale 500	10	6	497	Running	10,650
	Darlington–TranSouth 500	1	4	367	Running	52,250
	North Wilkesboro–First Union 400	1	5	400	Running	38,550
	Martinsville–Sovran Bank 500	21	3	347	DNF–Engine	9,915
	Talladega–Winston 500	2	14	188	Running	53,900
	Dover–Budweiser 500	3	2	499	Running	24,900
	Charlotte–Coca-Cola 600	1	3	400	Running	98,150
	Riverside–Budweiser 400	5	10	95	Running	14,125
	Pocono–Miller High Life 500	2	8	200	Running	29,750
	Michigan–Miller American 400	6	11	200	Running	17,650
	Daytona–Firecracker 400	27	5	151	DNF–Crash	14,895
	Pocono–Summer 500	7	10	150	Running	14,655
	Talladega–Talladega 500	26	2	153	DNF–Engine	15,355
	Watkins Glen–The Bud at the Glen	3	10	90	Running	25,250
	Michigan–Champion Spark Plug 400	5	12	199	Running	18,750
	Bristol–Busch 500	4	5	499	Running	12,800
	Darlington–Southern 500	9	21	366	Running	15,735
	Richmond–Wrangler Jeans Indigo 400	2	5	400	Running	24,525
	Dover–Delaware 500	21	3	432	Running	10,750
	Martinsville–Goody's 500	12	2	494	Running	11,770
	North Wilkesboro–Holly Farms 400	9	14	398	Running	9,500
	Charlotte–Oakwood Homes 500	1	3	334	Running	82,050
	Rockingham–Nationwise 500	6	10	491	Running	15,750
	Atlanta–Atlanta Journal 500	1	4	328	Running	67,950
	Riverside–Winston Western 500	2	8	119	Running	26,750
1987	Daytona–Daytona 500	5	13	200	Running	64,925
	Rockingham–Goodwrench 500	1	14	492	Running	53,900
	Richmond–Miller High Life 400	1	3	400	Running	49,150
	Atlanta–Motorcraft Quality Parts 500	16	1	322	Running	19,520
	Darlington–TranSouth 500	1	2	367	Running	52,985
	North Wilkesboro–First Union 400	1	3	400	Running	44,675
	Bristol–Valleydale Meats 500	1	3	500	Running	43,850
	Martinsville–Sovran Bank 500	1	4	500	Running	50,850
	Talladega–Winston 500	4	5	178	Running	31,350
	Charlotte–Coca-Cola 600	20	3	305	Running	19,600
	Dover–Budweiser 500	4	10	498	Running	20,775
	Pocono–Miller High Life 500	5	7	200	Running	22,400
	Riverside–Budweiser 400	7	8	95	Running	13,500
	Michigan–Miller American 400	1	5	200	Running	60,250
	Daytona–Pepsi Firecracker 400	6	13	160	Running	22,160
	Pocono–Summer 500	1	16	200	Running	55,875
	Talladega–Talladega 500	3	2	188	Running	35,050
	Watkins Glen–The Bud at the Glen	8	11	90	Running	17,005

Year	Race	Finish	Start	Laps Completed	Condition	Money
	Michigan–Champion Spark Plug 400	2	8	200	Running	34,325
	Bristol–Busch 500	1	6	500	Running	47,175
	Darlington–Southern 500	1	5	202	Running	64,650
	Richmond–Wrangler Jeans Indigo 400	1	8	400	Running	44,950
	Dover–Delaware 500	31	22	304	DNF–Engine	12,700
	Martinsville–Goody's 500	2	8	500	Running	29,875
	North Wilkesboro–Holly Farms 400	2	10	400	Running	26,950
	Charlotte–Oakwood Homes 500	12	9	329	Running	16,440
	Rockingham–AC Delco 500	2	2	492	Running	38,915
	Riverside–Winston Western 500	30	8	93	DNF–Engine	11,975
	Atlanta–Atlanta Journal 500	2	2	328	Running	35,350
	Daytona–Daytona 500	10	6	200	Running	52,540
1988	Richmond–Pontiac Excitement 400	10	2	399	Running	16,245
	Rockingham–Goodwrench 500	5	22	492	Running	19,865
	Atlanta–Motorcraft Quality Parts 500	1	2	328	Running	67,950
	Darlington–TranSouth 500	11	2	363	Running	14,825
	Bristol–Valleydale Meats 500	14	4	461	Running	12,050
	North Wilkesboro–First Union 400	3	10	400	Running	22,115
	Martinsville–Pannill Sweatshirts 500	1	14	500	Running	53,550
	Talladega–Winston 500	9	16	188	Running	21,500
	Charlotte–Coca-Cola 600	13	7	394	Running	19,205
	Dover–Budweiser 500	16	9	495	Running	13,450
	Riverside–Budweiser 400	4	6	95	Running	18,600
	Pocono–Miller High Life 500	33	18	93	DNF–Engine	13,045
	Michigan–Miller High Life 400	4	9	200	Running	26,175
	Daytona–Pepsi Firecracker 400	4	20	160	Running	22,825
	Pocono–AC Spark Plug 500	11	9	200	Running	15,025
	Talladega–Talladega DieHard 500	3	6	188	Running	37,775
	Watkins Glen–The Bud at the Glen	6	19	90	Running	18,530
	Michigan–Champion Spark Plug 400	29	5	194	Running	14,315
	Bristol–Busch 500	1	5	500	Running	48,500
	Darlington–Southern 500	3	2	367	Running	31,375
	Richmond–Miller High Life 400	2	19	400	Running	29,625
	Dover–Delaware 500	2	12	500	Running	37,450
	Martinsville–Goody's 500	8	10	498	Running	13,050
	Charlotte–Oakwood Homes 500	17	11	328	Running	24,300
	North Wilkesboro–Holly Farms 400	6	22	400	Running	15,475
	Rockingham–AC Delco 500	5	13	491	Running	27,965
	Phoenix–Checker 500	11	13	311	Running	15,100
	Atlanta–Atlanta Journal 500	14	2	326	Running	16,750
1989	Daytona–Daytona 500	3	8	200	Running	95,550
	Rockingham–Goodwrench 500	3	19	492	Running	24,200
	Atlanta–Motorcraft Quality Parts 500	2	5	328	Running	39,675
	Richmond–Pontiac Excitement 400	3	6	400	Running	30,900
	Darlington–TranSouth 500	33	11	290	Running	10,655
	Bristol–Valleydale Meats 500	16	5	492	Running	21,280
	North Wilkesboro–First Union 400	1	3	400	Running	51,225
	Martinsville–Pannill Sweatshirts 500	2	7	500	Running	34,525
	Talladega–Winston 500	8	17	188	Running	20,450
	Charlotte–Coca-Cola 600	38	14	223	DNF–Engine	10,750
	Dover–Budweiser 500	1	2	500	Running	59,350
	Sears Point–Banquet Frozen Foods 300	4	10	74	Running	20,350
	Pocono–Miller High Life 500	3	7	200	Running	29,250
	Michigan–Miller High Life 400	17	6	198	Running	13,775
	Daytona–Pepsi 400	18	13	158	Running	13,180
	Pocono–AC Spark Plug 500	9	3	200	Running	14,275
	Talladega–Talladega DieHard 500	11	9	188	Running	15,020
	Watkins Glen–The Bud at the Glen	3	4	90	Running	38,140
	Michigan–Champion Spark Plug 400	17	15	198	Running	13,450
	Bristol–Busch 500	14	7	490	Running	11,650
	Darlington–Heinz Southern 500	1	10	367	Running	71,150
	Richmond–Miller High Life 400	2	8	400	Running	31,475
	Dover–Peak Performance 500	1	15	500	Running	59,950
	Martinsville–Goody's 500	9	1	499	Running	15,950
	Charlotte–All Pro Auto Parts 500	42	12	13	DNF–Mechanical	11,250
	North Wilkesboro–Holly Farms 400	10	1	400	Running	15,155
	Rockingham–AC Delco 500	20	5	484	Running	13,775
	Phoenix–Autoworks 500	6	7	312	Running	16,995
	Atlanta–Atlanta Journal 500	1	3	328	Running	81,700

Year	Race	Finish	Start	Laps Completed	Condition	Money
1990	Daytona–Daytona 500	5	2	200	Running	109,325
	Richmond–Pontiac Excitement 400	2	4	400	Running	42,600
	Rockingham–GM Goodwrench 500	10	4	489	Running	17,150
	Atlanta–Motorcraft Quality Parts 500	1	1	328	Running	85,000
	Darlington–TranSouth 500	1	15	367	Running	61,985
	Bristol–Valleydale Meats 500	19	9	451	Running	10,990
	North Wilkesboro–First Union 400	3	4	400	Running	21,775
	Martinsville–Hanes Activewear 500	5	2	499	Running	20,800
	Talladega–Winston 500	1	5	188	Running	98,975
	Charlotte–Coca-Cola 600	30	12	262	Running	13,950
	Dover–Budweiser 500	31	4	159	DNF–Engine	12,600
	Sears Point–Banquet Frozen Foods 300	34	3	65	Running	12,650
	Pocono–Miller Genuine Draft 500	13	6	200	Running	14,150
	Michigan–Miller Genuine Draft 400	1	5	200	Running	72,950
	Daytona–Pepsi 400	1	3	160	Running	72,850
	Pocono–AC Spark Plug 500	4	11	200	Running	22,800
	Talladega–DieHard 500	1	1	188	Running	152,975
	Watkins Glen–The Bud at the Glen	7	1	90	Running	22,380
	Michigan–Champion Spark Plug 400	8	7	200	Running	19,400
	Bristol–Busch 500	8	1	499	Running	30,125
	Darlington–Heinz Southern 500	1	1	367	Running	210,350
	Richmond–Miller Genuine Draft 400	1	6	400	Running	59,225
	Dover–Peak AntiFreeze 500	3	3	500	Running	29,375
	Martinsville–Goody's 500	2	8	500	Running	30,550
	North Wilkesboro–Tyson/Holly Farms 400	2	8	400	Running	32,075
	Charlotte–Mello Yello 500	25	15	320	Running	12,275
	Rockingham–AC Delco 500	10	20	490	Running	19,750
	Phoenix–Checker 500	1	3	312	Running	72,100
	Atlanta–Atlanta Journal 500	3	6	328	Running	26,700
1991	Daytona–Daytona 500 by STP	5	4	200	Running	113,850
	Richmond–Pontiac Excitement 400	1	19	400	Running	67,950
	Rockingham–GM Goodwrench 500	8	13	489	Running	18,850
	Atlanta–Motorcraft Quality Parts 500	3	21	328	Running	37,000
	Darlington–TranSouth 500	29	7	332	DNF–Mechanical	14,310
	Bristol–Valleydale Meats 500	20	2	484	Running	15,525
	North Wilkesboro–First Union 400	2	17	400	Running	35,225
	Martinsville–Hanes 500	1	10	500	Running	63,600
	Talladega–Winston 500	3	8	188	Running	56,100
	Charlotte–Coca-Cola 600	3	14	400	Running	53,650
	Dover–Budweiser 500	2	10	500	Running	44,275
	Sears Point–Banquet Frozen Foods 300	7	3	74	Running	14,400
	Pocono–Champion Spark Plug 500	2	21	200	Running	43,775
	Michigan–Miller Genuine Draft 400	4	6	200	Running	30,950
	Daytona–Pepsi 400	7	12	160	Running	23,200
	Pocono–Miller Genuine Draft 500	22	16	175	Running	15,350
	Talladega–DieHard 500	1	4	188	Running	88,670
	Watkins Glen–The Bud at the Glen	15	8	90	Running	16,180
	Michigan–Champion Spark Plug 400	24	26	194	Running	16,425
	Bristol–Bud 500	7	13	498	Running	16,025
	Darlington–Heinz Southern 500	8	3	365	Running	20,470
	Richmond–Miller Genuine Draft 400	11	16	398	Running	13,750
	Dover–Peak AntiFreeze 500	15	12	447	Running	16,700
	Martinsville–Goody's 500	3	5	500	Running	30,350
	North Wilkesboro–Tyson/Holly Farms 400	1	16	400	Running	69,350
	Charlotte–Mello Yello 500	25	15	302	DNF–Mechanical	22,460
	Rockingham–AC Delco 500	7	4	490	Running	19,250
	Phoenix–Pyroil 500	9	12	311	Running	18,200
	Atlanta–Hardee's 500	5	5	328	Running	27,825
1992	Daytona–Daytona 500 by STP	9	3	199	Running	87,000
	Rockingham–GM Goodwrench 500	24	8	469	Running	16,850
	Richmond–Pontiac Excitement 400	11	29	399	Running	16,600
	Atlanta–Motorcraft Quality Parts 500	3	7	328	Running	36,850
	Darlington–TranSouth 500	10	8	365	Running	20,570
	Bristol–Food City 500	18	18	471	Running	18,130
	North Wilkesboro–First Union 400	6	9	400	Running	32,540
	Martinsville–Hanes 500	9	2	497	Running	22,550
	Talladega–Winston 500	3	10	188	Running	46,970
	Charlotte–Coca-Cola 600	1	13	400	Running	125,100
	Dover–Budweiser 500	2	24	500	Running	43,720

Year	Race	Finish	Start	Laps Completed	Condition	Money
	Sears Point–Save Mart 300K	6	12	74	Running	21,910
	Pocono–Champion Spark Plug 500	28	17	148	DNF–Engine	16,600
	Michigan–Miller Genuine Draft 400	9	22	199	Running	23,110
	Daytona–Pepsi 400	40	22	7	DNF–Engine	16,355
	Pocono–Miller Genuine Draft 500	23	29	199	Running	16,540
	Talladega–DieHard 500	40	30	52	DNF–Engine	18,140
	Watkins Glen–The Bud at the Glen	9	1	51	Running	22,430
	Michigan–Champion Spark Plug 400	16	41	199	Running	19,665
	Bristol–Bud 500	2	23	500	Running	39,325
	Darlington–Mountain Dew Southern 500	29	13	241	Running	16,555
	Richmond–Miller Genuine Draft 400	4	11	400	Running	29,655
	Dover–Peak AntiFreeze 500	21	5	470	Running	17,880
	Martinsville–Goody's 500	31	11	111	DNF–Engine	14,550
	North Wilkesboro–Tyson/Holly Farms 400	19	13	395	Running	15,350
	Charlotte–Mello Yello 500	14	11	332	Running	19,050
	Rockingham–AC Delco 500	8	12	490	Running	22,350
	Phoenix–Pyroil 500	10	19	311	Running	21,370
	Atlanta–Hooters 500	26	3	299	Running	20,670
1993	Daytona–Daytona 500 by STP	2	4	200	Running	181,825
	Rockingham–GM Goodwrench 500	2	7	492	Running	47,585
	Richmond–Pontiac Excitement 400	10	11	399	Running	17,000
	Atlanta–Motorcraft Quality Parts 500	11	2	325	Running	15,595
	Darlington–TranSouth 500	1	1	367	Running	64,815
	Bristol–Food City 500	2	6	500	Running	47,760
	North Wilkesboro–First Union 400	16	21	396	Running	13,130
	Martinsville–Hanes 500	22	21	453	DNF–Engine	10,625
	Talladega–Winston 500	4	1	188	Running	39,870
	Sears Point–Save Mart Supermarket 300K	6	1	74	Running	27,790
	Charlotte–Coca-Cola 600	1	14	400	Running	156,650
	Dover–Budweiser 500	1	8	500	Running	68,030
	Pocono–Champion Spark Plug 500	11	5	200	Running	14,815
	Michigan–Miller Genuine Draft 400	14	6	199	Running	16,385
	Daytona–Pepsi 400	1	5	160	Running	75,940
	New Hampshire–Slick 50 300	26	24	296	Running	15,300
	Pocono–Miller Genuine Draft 500	1	11	200	Running	66,795
	Talladega–DieHard 500	1	11	188	Running	87,315
	Watkins Glen–Bud at the Glen	18	5	90	Running	13,510
	Michigan–Champion Spark Plug 400	9	7	200	Running	19,215
	Bristol–Bud 500	3	19	500	Running	32,325
	Darlington–Mountain Dew Southern 500	4	6	351	Running	31,090
	Richmond–Miller Genuine Draft 400	3	8	400	Running	35,780
	Dover–SplitFire Spark Plug 500	27	9	404	Running	14,555
	Martinsville–Goody's 500	29	7	440	DNF–Mechanical	10,525
	North Wilkesboro–Tyson/Holly Farms 400	2	10	400	Running	46,285
	Charlotte–Mello Yello 500	3	9	334	Running	56,900
	Rockingham–AC Delco 500	2	22	492	Running	49,550
	Phoenix–Slick 50 500	4	11	312	Running	29,980
	Atlanta–Hooters 500	10	19	327	Running	19,300
1994	Daytona–Daytona 500	7	2	200	Running	110,340
	Rockingham–Goodwrench 500	7	19	491	Running	25,785
	Richmond–Pontiac Excitement 400	4	9	400	Running	29,550
	Atlanta–Purolator 500	12	16	325	Running	24,550
	Darlington–TranSouth Financial 400	1	9	293	Running	70,190
	Bristol–Food City 500	1	24	500	Running	72,570
	North Wilkesboro–First Union 400	5	19	400	Running	26,740
	Martinsville–Hanes 500	11	8	499	Running	21,060
	Talladega–Winston Select 500	1	4	188	Running	94,865
	Sears Point–Save Mart Supermarkets 300	3	4	74	Running	37,825
	Charlotte–Coca-Cola 600	9	24	397	Running	37,950
	Dover–Budweiser 500	28	14	425	Running	22,065
	Pocono–UAW-GM Teamwork 500	2	19	200	Running	46,425
	Michigan–Miller Genuine Draft 400	2	24	200	Running	55,905
	Daytona–Pepsi 400	3	1	160	Running	50,050
	New Hampshire–Slick 50 300	2	28	300	Running	68,000
	Pocono–Miller Genuine Draft 500	7	20	200	Running	26,210
	Talladega–DieHard 500	34	1	80	DNF–Engine	30,725
	Indianapolis–Brickyard 400	5	2	160	Running	121,625
	Watkins Glen–The Bud at the Glen	3	6	90	Running	39,605
	Michigan–GM Goodwrench Dealer 400	37	11	54	DNF–Crash	22,915

Year	Race	Finish	Start	Laps Completed	Condition	Money
	Bristol–Goody's 500	3	14	500	Running	33,265
	Darlington–Mountain Dew Southern 500	2	27	367	Running	45,030
	Richmond–Miller Genuine Draft 400	3	12	400	Running	38,830
	Dover–SplitFire Spark Plug 500	2	37	500	Running	47,980
	Martinsville–Goody's 500	2	20	500	Running	42,400
	North Wilkesboro–Tyson Holly Farms 400	7	3	398	Running	21,315
	Charlotte–Mello Yello 500	3	38	334	Running	66,000
	Rockingham–AC Delco 500	1	20	492	Running	60,600
	Phoenix–Slick 50 500	40	8	91	DNF–Engine	19,575
	Atlanta–Hooters 500	2	30	328	Running	55,950
1995	Daytona–Daytona 500	2	2	200	Running	269,750
	Rockingham–Goodwrench 500	3	23	492	Running	40,740
	Richmond–Pontiac Excitement 400	2	26	400	Running	57,200
	Atlanta–Purolator 500	4	1	328	Running	52,950
	Darlington–TranSouth Financial 400	2	23	293	Running	54,355
	Bristol–Food City 500	25	25	479	Running	36,360
	North Wilkesboro–First Union 400	1	5	400	Running	77,400
	Martinsville–Hanes 500	29	20	331	Running	27,515
	Talladega–Winston Select 500	21	16	188	Running	34,735
	Sears Point–Save Mart Supermarkets 300	1	4	74	Running	74,860
	Charlotte–Coca-Cola 600	6	34	399	Running	52,500
	Dover–Miller Genuine Draft 500	5	23	500	Running	45,545
	Pocono–UAW-GM Teamwork 500	8	24	200	Running	32,455
	Michigan–Miller Genuine Draft 400	35	7	127	DNF–Crash	29,945
	Daytona–Pepsi 400	3	1	160	Running	66,200
	New Hampshire–Slick 50 300	22	18	298	Running	43,350
	Pocono–Miller Genuine Draft 500	20	5	199	Running	31,555
	Talladega–DieHard 500	3	5	188	Running	57,105
	Indianapolis–Brickyard 400	1	13	160	Running	565,600
	Watkins Glen–The Bud at the Glen	23	15	89	Running	30,890
	Michigan–GM Goodwrench Dealer 400	35	8	87	DNF–Mechanical	29,965
	Bristol–Goody's 500	2	7	500	Running	66,890
	Darlington–Mountain Dew Southern 500	2	3	367	Running	62,155
	Richmond–Miller Genuine Draft 400	3	1	400	Running	54,005
	Dover–MBNA 500	5	28	500	Running	40,970
	Martinsville–Goody's 500	1	2	500	Running	78,150
	North Wilkesboro–Tyson/Holly Farms 400	9	13	399	Running	27,850
	Charlotte–UAW-GM Quality 500	2	43	334	Running	86,800
	Rockingham–AC Delco 400	7	20	393	Running	34,050
	Phoenix–Dura-Lube 500	3	2	312	Running	49,105
	Atlanta–NAPA 500	1	11	328	Running	141,850
1996	Daytona–Daytona 500	2	1	200	Running	215,065
	Rockingham–Goodwrench Service 400	1	18	393	Running	83,840
	Richmond–Pontiac Excitement 400	31	9	393	Running	27,265
	Atlanta–Purolator 500	1	18	328	Running	91,050
	Darlington–TranSouth Financial 400	14	27	292	Running	28,080
	Bristol–Food City 500	4	19	342	Running	35,351
	North Wilkesboro–First Union 400	3	26	400	Running	38,525
	Martinsville–Goody's Headache Powder 500	5	8	500	Running	35,195
	Talladega–Winston Select 500	3	16	188	Running	64,620
	Sears Point–Save Mart Supermarkets 300	4	5	74	Running	39,160
	Charlotte–Coca-Cola 600	2	20	400	Running	97,000
	Dover–Miller 500	3	14	500	Running	60,080
	Pocono–UAW-GM Teamwork 500	32	10	135	DNF–Engine	26,035
	Michigan–Miller 400	9	11	200	Running	33,350
	Daytona–Pepsi 400	4	7	117	Running	97,960
	New Hampshire–Jiffy Lube 300	12	5	300	Running	32,225
	Pocono–Miller 500	14	8	199	Running	27,925
	Talladega–DieHard 500	28	4	117	DNF–Crash	31,020
	Indianapolis–Brickyard 400	15	12	160	Running	84,460
	Watkins Glen–The Bud at the Glen	6	1	90	Running	52,960
	Michigan–GM Goodwrench Dealer 400	17	16	200	Running	32,865
	Bristol–Goody's Headache Powder 500	24	23	476	Running	32,310
	Darlington–Mountain Dew Southern 500	12	12	365	Running	30,545
	Richmond–Miller 400	20	23	398	Running	30,100
	Dover–MBNA 500	16	20	498	Running	31,515
	Martinsville–Hanes 500	15	19	498	Running	29,100
	North Wilkesboro–Tyson Holly Farms 400	2	11	400	Running	51,940
	Charlotte–UAW-GM Quality 500	6	34	334	Running	44,700

Year	Race	Finish	Start	Laps Completed	Condition	Money
	Rockingham–AC Delco 400	9	15	393	Running	30,700
	Phoenix–Dura-Lube 500	12	24	312	Running	29,055
	Atlanta–NAPA 500	4	17	328	Running	47,400
1997	Daytona–Daytona 500	31	4	195	Running	72,545
	Rockingham–Goodwrench Service 400	11	27	393	Running	32,000
	Richmond–Pontiac Excitement 400	25	4	397	Running	27,940
	Atlanta–Primestar 500	8	26	328	Running	40,975
	Darlington–TranSouth Financial 400	15	43	292	Running	28,625
	Texas–Interstate Batteries 500	6	15	334	Running	111,700
	Bristol–Food City 500	6	29	500	Running	32,970
	Martinsville–Goody's Headache Powder 500	12	25	500	Running	28,400
	Sears Point–SaveMart Supermarkets 300	12	32	74	Running	39,580
	Talladega–Winston 500	2	3	188	Running	85,445
	Charlotte–Coca-Cola 600	7	33	333	Running	54,400
	Dover–Miller 500	16	43	497	Running	33,265
	Pocono–Pocono 500	10	12	200	Running	34,025
	Michigan–Miller 400	7	22	200	Running	41,375
	California–California 500	16	14	249	Running	41,975
	Daytona–Pepsi 400	4	2	160	Running	52,475
	New Hampshire–Jiffy Lube 300	2	26	300	Running	82,950
	Pocono–Pennsylvania 500	12	5	200	Running	29,490
	Indianapolis–Brickyard 400	29	5	158	Running	76,310
	Watkins Glen–Bud at the Glen	16	3	90	Running	29,575
	Michigan–DeVilbiss 400	9	28	200	Running	37,940
	Bristol–Goody's Headache Powder 500	14	34	497	Running	32,515
	Darlington–Mountain Dew Southern 500	30	36	282	Running	30,925
	Richmond–Exide 400	15	22	398	Running	33,775
	New Hampshire–CMT 300	8	30	300	Running	49,025
	Dover–MBNA 400	2	33	400	Running	63,105
	Martinsville–Hanes 500	2	13	500	Running	65,800
	Charlotte–UAW-GM Quality 500	3	19	334	Running	85,650
	Talladega–DieHard 500	29	12	167	Running	48,500
	Rockingham–AC Delco 400	8	26	393	Running	32,800
	Phoenix–Dura-Lube 500	5	7	312	Running	39,300
	Atlanta–NAPA 500	16	6	322	Running	43,075
1998	Daytona–Daytona 500	1	4	200	Running	1,059,105
	Rockingham–GM Goodwrench Service Plus 400	17	37	392	Running	32,100
	Las Vegas–Las Vegas 400	8	26	267	Running	84,500
	Atlanta–Primestar 500	13	30	324	Running	39,055
	Darlington–TranSouth Financial 400	12	27	292	Running	37,595
	Bristol–Food City 500	22	37	496	Running	33,715
	Texas–Texas 500	35	34	205	Running	58,200
	Martinsville–Goody's Headache Powder 500	4	31	500	Running	49,475
	Talladega–Diehard 500	36	2	144	DNF–Crash	38,250
	California–California 500	9	43	250	Running	53,800
	Charlotte–Coca-Cola 600	39	28	336	DNF–Crash	39,580
	Dover–MBNA Platinum 400	25	34	395	Running	33,205
	Richmond–Pontiac Excitement 400	21	38	398	Running	34,250
	Michigan–Miller Lite 400	15	25	199	Running	38,650
	Pocono–Pocono 500	8	11	200	Running	34,625
	Sears Point–Save Mart/Kragen 350	11	17	112	Running	44,950
	New Hampshire–Jiffy Lube 300	18	20	299	Running	47,150
	Pocono–Pennsylvania 500	7	9	200	Running	49,890
	Indianapolis–Brickyard 400	5	28	160	Running	169,275
	Watkins Glen–The Bud at the Glen	11	22	90	Running	36,355
	Michigan–Pepsi 400	18	37	198	Running	34,840
	Bristol–Goody's Headache Powder 500	6	30	500	Running	42,540
	New Hampshire–Farm Aid on CMT 300	9	18	300	Running	50,550
	Darlington–Mountain Dew Southern 500	4	18	367	Running	64,465
	Richmond–Exide Batteries 400	38	34	260	Running	34,495
	Dover–MBNA Gold 400	23	43	396	Running	32,140
	Martinsville–NAPA Autocare 500	22	33	495	Running	32,950
	Charlotte–UAW-GM Quality 500	29	33	278	Running	31,300
	Talladega–Winston 500	32	14	175	DNF–Mechanical	40,920
	Daytona–Pepsi 400	10	5	160	Running	57,375
	Phoenix–Dura Lube/KMart 500	3	39	257	Running	57,175
	Rockingham–AC Delco 400	9	29	393	Running	34,400
	Atlanta–NAPA 500	13	37	221	Running	46,025

Year	Race	Finish	Start	Laps Completed	Condition	Money
1999	Daytona–Daytona 500	2	4	200	Running	613,659
	Rockingham–Dura-Lube/Big Kmart 400	41	18	275	DNF–Crash	36,725
	Las Vegas–Las Vegas 400	7	38	267	Running	91,350
	Atlanta–Cracker Barrel Old Country Store 500	40	33	151	DNF–Mechanical	41,625
	Darlington–TranSouth Financial 400	25	30	163	Running	37,020
	Texas–Primestar 500	8	38	334	Running	97,775
	Bristol–Food City 500	10	34	500	Running	48,630
	Martinsville–Goody's Body Pain 500	19	39	498	Running	39,150
	Talladega–Diehard 500	1	17	188	Running	147,795
	California–California 500	12	9	249	Running	55,425
	Richmond–Pontiac Excitement 400	8	37	400	Running	48,540
	Charlotte–Coca-Cola 600	6	15	400	Running	70,225
	Dover–MBNA Platinum 400	11	34	398	Running	49,510
	Michigan–Kmart 400	16	15	198	Running	39,825
	Pocono–Pocono 500	7	25	200	Running	57,190
	Sears Point–Save Mart/Kragen 350K	9	23	112	Running	46,165
	Daytona–Pepsi 400	2	10	160	Running	92,175
	New Hampshire–Jiffy Lube 300	8	14	300	Running	56,675
	Pocono–Pennsylvania 500	9	11	200	Running	48,765
	Indianapolis–Brickyard 400	10	18	160	Running	135,525
	Watkins Glen–Frontier at the Glen	20	14	90	Running	41,525
	Michigan–Pepsi 400	5	38	200	Running	51,005
	Bristol–Goody's Headache Powder 500	1	26	500	Running	89,880
	Darlington–Pepsi Southern 500	22	25	268	Running	42,470
	Richmond–Exide Batteries 400	6	33	400	Running	47,055
	New Hampshire–Dura-Lube/Kmart 300	13	16	300	Running	55,125
	Dover–MBNA Gold 400	8	37	399	Running	52,065
	Martinsville–NAPA AutoCare 500	2	38	500	Running	70,225
	Charlotte–UAW-GM Quality 500	12	17	332	Running	44,450
	Talladega–Winston 500	1	27	188	Running	120,290
	Rockingham–Pop Secret Popcorn 400	40	37	318	DNF–Crash	36,900
	Phoenix–Checker Auto Parts/Dura-Lube 500K	11	14	312	Running	57,225
	Homestead–Pennzoil 400	8	23	266	Running	65,575
	Atlanta–NAPA 500	9	36	325	Running	54,550
2000	Daytona–Daytona 500	21	21	200	Running	116,075
	Rockingham–Dura Lube/Kmart 400	2	4	393	Running	78,610
	Las Vegas–Carsdirect.com 400	8	33	148	Running	94,900
	Atlanta–Cracker Barrel Old Country Store 500	1	35	325	Running	123,100
	Darlington–Mall.com 400	3	4	293	Running	68,590
	Bristol–Food City 500	39	11	346	Running	45,215
	Texas–DirecTV 500	7	17	334	Running	108,750
	Martinsville–Goody's Body Pain 500	9	17	500	Running	48,550
	Talladega–DieHard 500	3	4	188	Running	92,630
	California–NAPA Auto Parts 500	17	35	250	Running	59,075
	Richmond–Pontiac Excitement 400	10	31	400	Running	52,800
	Charlotte–Coca-Cola 600	3	15	400	Running	103,250
	Dover–MBNA Platinum 400	6	30	399	Running	75,455
	Michigan–Kmart 400	2	9	194	Running	80,575
	Pocono–Pocono 500	4	16	200	Running	87,495
	Sears Point–Save Mart/Kragen 300	6	29	112	Running	65,165
	Daytona–Pepsi 400	8	18	160	Running	64,375
	New Hampshire–New England 300	6	24	273	Running	69,425
	Pocono–Pennsylvania 500	25	25	199	Running	48,915
	Indianapolis–Brickyard 400	8	8	160	Running	143,510
	Watkins Glen–Global Crossing at The Glen	25	3	90	Running	45,180
	Michigan–Pepsi 400	6	37	200	Running	51,190
	Bristol–Goracing.com 500	4	17	500	Running	62,980
	Darlington–Southern 500	3	6	328	Running	82,745
	Richmond–Chevrolet Monte Carlo 400	2	22	400	Running	81,190
	New Hampshire–New Hampsire 300	12	37	299	Running	62,550
	Dover–MBNA.com 400	17	37	398	Running	63,390
	Martinsville–NAPA AutoCare 500	2	12	500	Running	77,925
	Charlotte–UAW-GM Quality 500	11	37	334	Running	58,750
	Talladega–Winston 500	1	20	188	Running	1,135,900
	Rockingham–Pop Secret 400	17	27	393	Running	46,625
	Phoenix–Checker Auto Parts/DuraLube 500K	9	31	312	Running	69,300
	Homestead–Pennzoil 400	20	37	264	Running	60,700
	Atlanta–NAPA 500	2	8	325	Running	99,750
2001	Daytona–Daytona 500	12	7	199	DNF–Crash	194,111

INDEX